Endorsements

Some days it seems impossible to find a moment to be still and know that He is God, and yet how vital it is that we do so. *Be Still...and Let Your Nail Polish Dry* is a devotional that will help you center your thoughts on the Maker of the Universe and remind you to be thankful for His loving care in every moment of your life.
—**Robin Lee Hatcher, Author of** *A Vote of Confidence* **and** *The Perfect Life*

* * *

Let's talk busy! Between a husband, three children, three dogs, a new television show, and sharing my faith at churches across the country, I barely found the time to write a note of endorsement! Then it hit me, and I giggled.... This is the *perfect* devotional for me. My day just isn't right if it doesn't start out with prayer to the Lord. But sometimes waking up at 4:30 a.m. to get in Bible study time before my day starts just isn't realistic. *Be Still...and Let Your Nail Polish Dry* is a modern, fun, and easy-to-read devotional, giving us God's Word to chew on whether we're sitting in the school carpool line or taking the next flight out for a business trip. Carry this devotional in your purse or leave it in your car to make the most of those five-minute periods of quiet time to spend with the Lord. You'll be so happy you did.
—**Candace Cameron-Bure, Actress, Public Speaker, Wife, and Mom**

* * *

Be Still...and Let Your Nail Polish Dry is a book every busy Christian woman needs to pick up! The devotionals are short yet meaningful and relevant. I believe it will bring you closer in your walk with the Lord, as it has me.
—**Tammy Trent, Recording Artist, Speaker, and Author of** *Learning to Breathe Again*

* * *

Be Still...and Let Your Nail Polish Dry is a book that uses the writers' Christian beliefs to guide the reader through difficult situations. Fear. Loss. Pain. The unexplained. The myriad challenges we face every day. I encourage you to read these stories to help you understand how to accept those situations we cannot change. To find comfort.
—**Elizabeth Howard, CEO of the Ovarian Cancer Research Fund**

A *Devo* for Women on the Go!

Be Still...
and Let Your Nail Polish Dry

Andrea Boeshaar ✳ Sandra D. Bricker
Loree Lough ✳ Debby Mayne

summerside
PRESS

Be Still...and Let Your Nail Polish Dry © 2008 by Andrea Boeshaar, Sandra D. Bricker, Loree Lough, and Debby Mayne

ISBN 978-1-935416-21-0

Cover and interior design by Greg Jackson and Nathan Pyles of Thinkpen Design | thinkpendesign.com. Typesetting by James Baker of James Baker Design | jamesbakerdesign.com.

Published by Summerside Press, Inc., Minneapolis, MN. 55337 | www.summersidepress.com. Summerside Press™ is an inspirational publisher offering fresh, irresistible books to uplift the heart and engage the mind.

Printed in China.

Dedication

To Connie Troyer, "editer"

In the great words of Loree Lough,
"Yer a peach!"
Although Andrea thinks yer more of a blueberry.
And Debby says yer definitely a pomegranate.
But Sandie insists yer a sweet little seedless grape.

With thanks "fer" all the late nights
and Goldfish cravings
and eyestrain.

Introduction

Proverbs 31 describes the life of a woman in biblical times. She worked with her hands; she rose early to provide food for her family; she employed servants, bought land, and worked out to keep her body strong; she helped the poor, operated a business, spoke wisely, and tried to be kind. She was seldom idle. We're exhausted just thinking about it!

But the truth is...that woman isn't so different from us.

Centuries later we don't make our own clothes, but we do spend time shopping for them at a discount. And we don't weave our own tapestries—but we make costumes for the school play, drive carpools, and volunteer our time. And we're just as exhausted at the end of our days.

Like those women, we are commanded to spend time communing with God: "Be still, and know that I am God" (Psalm 46:10 NIV).

And we mean to, we really do. How many New Year's resolutions include the promise to take time in the Word each and every day? And when February rolls in, how many of us are still managing that?

What if we resolved to spend a few minutes in the Word twice a week? That might be doable, right? And what if we had a devotional written just for busy women like us, with two devotions per week, spread out over an entire year? Would we be more likely to follow through on our commitment? We think so, which is why we've written this book.

So make a promise to yourself: *My spiritual life will be added to the top of that growing list of priorities in my life. Here and now, I commit to reading from this book twice a week for the whole year. No matter if I'm in my car at the drive-thru, having my morning coffee, or giving myself a pedicure!*

That's the spirit! Now sit back, take a deep breath, sigh...and then take this journey with us over the course of the next year.

Just be still...*and let your nail polish dry.* We're with you, sistah!

Andrea, Sandie, Loree, and Debby

The Awesomest!

God is jealous.... The LORD is slow to anger and great in power....
The LORD has his way.... He rebukes the sea.... The LORD is good....

NAHUM 1:2–7 NKJV

I couldn't see the road ahead of me. The falling snow had covered it like a heavy drape. I couldn't tell where the road ended and the gravel shoulder began. I did, however, make out the ditch's location, since another vehicle had spun out and landed in it. The car's taillights flashed as its driver waited for a tow truck.

I clenched the steering wheel, and my shoulders tightened with tension. I prayed I wouldn't meet the same fate.

Illuminated by my headlights, white flakes zoomed in at me. I began to feel dizzy, like I'd gotten sucked into a snow globe and someone had just given it a good shake. I wondered if I'd make it home unharmed and with my minivan intact.

To quell my rising panic, I turned on the radio. I searched the FM band before finding the only Christian station whose signal was strong enough to reach me on this stormy night. An upbeat tune sung by Rich Mullins filled my vehicle. The words went something like: "When He rolls up His sleeves, He ain't just puttin' on the ritz.... There's thunder in His footsteps and lightning in His fists. Our God is an awesome God."

As I listened, I was reminded of what a Superhero Jesus Christ really is and how the Bible describes His awesomeness. God is jealous—He created us for fellowship with Him. He is slow to anger. He is of great power. He rebukes the sea (and blizzards too!). He has His way (Thy will be done). The Lord is good (Nahum 1:2–7).

Our God is an awesome God.

God is faithful and just to forgive... (1 John 1:9). God is love (1 John 4:8).

Our God is an awesome God.

By now my death grip on the steering wheel had loosened and my shoulders had relaxed. I wished I had started out on this trek remembering that God is in control always. He would see me through this storm.

I thought of another scripture verse: "God is our refuge and strength, a very present help in trouble" (Psalm 46:1 KJV).

Our God is an awesome God.

I came to an intersection and eased on the brake, slowing my van. I attempted a complete stop, but the road was too slippery and I slid right past the stoplight instead. The driver of a pickup truck, coming toward me on the right, miraculously saw me and swerved just in time.

Our God is an awesome God.

At long last, I left the country highway and turned onto my street. Moments later, I pulled into my driveway—safe from the storm.

Our God is most definitely an awesome God! ✳ *AKB*

Today's Prayer

Thank You, Father, for seeing us through the storms of life,
both great and small. Thank You for being the Hero of all heroes,
mighty and powerful. Great is Your faithfulness, Lord.
You truly are an awesome God.

A Toddler for Life

"Fear not, for I have redeemed you;
I have called you by your name; you are Mine.
When you pass through the waters, I will be with you;
and through the rivers, they shall not overflow you.
When you walk through the fire, you shall not be burned,
nor shall the flame scorch you."

ISAIAH 43:1–2 NKJV

I went to the beach with Chloe and her daughter, a wide-eyed toddler named Emma. The two-year-old was quite an independent thinker and surprisingly swift on her feet considering how short a time she'd actually been on them. Slathered in sunscreen, donning a pink hat with a large yellow sunflower, and negotiating each flip-flopped step, the child was fearless.

Chloe, however, followed along behind her daughter, slightly bent into a sort of catcher's stance, ready for whatever surprise might pop up. As Emma came upon a large hole in the sand, Chloe lifted the little girl over it and then set her down on the other side, and the child toddled forward without missing a beat. When the foamy surf sped across the sand toward Emma, Chloe swept her up into her arms above it and then set her safely down again, her feet still going a mile a minute, once the waters retreated.

As I watched them, I realized that they were a beautiful, sunshiny picture-type of how the Lord must feel about us our whole lives long. His Word says that He has called us by name, the way Chloe and her husband decided that "Emma" was just the perfect name for their smiling blue-eyed baby.

"Did you notice Emma's hair?" Chloe asked me that afternoon.

"I'm sorry. What about her hair?"

"She's got at least one hundred more strands than the last time you saw her!"

In the same way that Chloe keeps count of Emma's hairs and how many steps she can take in a row, the Lord also knows the number of hairs on our heads and how fast we'll trot directly into trouble. He keeps each of our tears in a bottle, and His love for us is endless in that perfect parental way. I so love that! When we head for the deeper waters, the Lord is there just like a well-prepared and loving parent to sweep us up in His arms and to make sure we're not overtaken. When the flames reach out toward us, He tosses Himself over us like a cloak so we're supernaturally protected and safe until the danger has passed.

Even in the times when the danger isn't entirely averted and we scrape a knee or an elbow or worse, our loving Father is bent behind us in a catcher's stance, ready and willing to hold us tight in His glove and walk through it with us.

The realization that, in that way, I can live the carefree, fearless existence of a toddler for the rest of my life is somehow comforting. And looking back throughout history at the Jonahs and the Peters and the Pauls, I'm really happy that my God has a gazillion years of catching practice! ✱ *SDB*

Today's Prayer

Thank You, Father, for Your protection and grace. Thank You for the assurance that nothing is going to happen to me today that You and I can't handle together. In Jesus' name I pray, amen.

The Right Note

I will praise the name of God with a song,
and will magnify him with thanksgiving.

PSALM 69:30 KJV

This morning when I woke, my sleep-deprived brain was serenading me with, "When I woke up this morning, you were on my mi–i–i–ind...." Which got me to thinking about all the other times I've opened my eyes and almost instantly started humming one tune or another. I've come to the conclusion that it's God's way of starting my day on the right note, literally. Even before I sit down at the kitchen table, with pen in hand to craft my latest to-do list, He has prepared my mind for the busy day ahead. Better still, He's prepared my heart, because, let's face it...with all that singing and humming, how can I help but leap into my chores with a happy spirit?

Like millions of other Christian women, demands on my time come from so many angles that I've often jokingly referred to my overcrowded calendar as the Diamond—because it has so many "facets." It doesn't matter if it's the vacuum cleaner, the dishwasher, or the laundry machine that's humming, because peripheral vision shows me a kitchen floor that needs to be washed, a dog to let out, a grocery list as-yet unshopped, and appointments to be made...or canceled. There are menus to plan and meals to prepare, bills to pay and a checkbook to balance. Cookies to bake for the church bazaar and my promise to visit Children's Oncology to paint cartoon characters on little bald patients.

Oh, but isn't it amazing how well the Lord knows me. Allowing me to start my days with song, even before my feet hit the floor, is such a gift that it brings tears to my eyes!

If your demanding schedule is growing heavy and burdensome, here's my advice to you:

As you whisper your bedtime prayers, ask the Father to wake you with a song. You'll find, as I do, that throughout the day, as you stop to catch your breath or wonder where you'll find that extra ounce of energy to check off yet another item from your too-long to-do list, the melody will echo in your head...and your heart won't be able to help but sing along.

And God doesn't care if you sing off-key! ✳ *LL*

Today's Prayer

O Lord, how I love You for meeting even the smallest of my needs.
I pray You'll continue reminding me there is music in every task I perform, in
every action I take, in every thought I conjure—for while I'm singing,
I'm always aware of how easy it is to praise Your name! Amen.

Be Prepared

And He said to me, "My grace is sufficient for you,
for My strength is made perfect in weakness."
Therefore most gladly I will rather boast in my infirmities,
that the power of Christ may rest upon me.

2 CORINTHIANS 12:9 NKJV

When I first got married, my husband resisted wearing seat belts for short jaunts—like to the store or the golf course. He reserved the car restraint for longer trips, with the notion that his risks were greater when he spent more time in the car. It took me awhile to convince him, but armed with research on how much more likely people were to get into accidents close to home than on long trips, he started clicking his seat belt every time he got in the car.

I think many of us live with the notion that precautions should only be taken under certain conditions—like saving seat belts for long trips or carrying an umbrella only when it's already pouring outside. When we start the day with sunny skies, we don't think about the importance of protection. However, when we walk out of our office at the end of a long day and it's pouring buckets, that umbrella sure would come in handy.

When life is going according to our plan, why do we need protection? I can't make many guarantees, but one thing I can promise is that eventually something will happen and you won't feel all smug about how nice and perfect things are. One of these days, you'll be glad you thought to click your seat belt or toss your umbrella into your bag before leaving the house.

This reminds me of how I used to live my Christian life. When things were going well, it was easy to leave Jesus on the back burner. I've even heard people say that they didn't "need" Him because they had a good life. The problem is, things happen. Imperfect people drive imperfect cars, and even if we don't get into an accident, seat belts can protect us when we have to slam on the brakes. If we have that umbrella in the car at all times, we're always protected. If we're armed with the gospel during the good times and the bad, we have the greatest protection of all. ✴ *DM*

Today's Prayer

As You lead me through the hazards of life, Lord,
hold me close and give me the strength I need.
Show me how to trust You through the power of Your Word. Amen.

Driving Lessons

*As soon as Jesus heard the word that was spoken,
He said to the ruler of the synagogue, "Do not be afraid; only believe."*

MARK 5:36 NKJV

Do you believe that God can keep you safe, even during life's scariest times?

I do. I taught my sons how to drive!

For parents, our children's driver's licenses are a benchmark in life that requires praying without ceasing as we're lying in bed at night, trying to fall asleep, while our young person is out driving the car. Time after time, the Lord had to remind me (and still does) that worrying is futile and faith is vital. During these times, I like to recite Philippians 4:6–7: "Be anxious for nothing, but in everything by prayer and supplication with thanksgiving let your requests be made known to God. And the peace of God, which surpasses all comprehension, will guard your hearts and your minds in Christ Jesus" (NASB). Then the Lord tells me, "Don't be afraid; only believe."

Believing and trusting are hard work because they involve a surrendering process—a giving-up of control. Like riding in the car with your teenager, who's sitting behind the steering wheel.

One of the most frightening experiences for me occurred when I rode in the backseat while my oldest son, Ben, drove. He had just earned his regular operator's license and wanted to drive home from church. He asked me to sit in the back so my middle son, Rick, could sit in the passenger seat—so they'd both look cool. I never knew such fear, sitting there in the backseat of my '88 black Ford Escort. But Ben and Rick sure did look cool.

"Slow down, Ben." I instructed with my heart pounding. "You're going too fast."

"Mom, the speed limit is 40, and I'm going 35."

"It feels like 75!" I gripped the side handle and my youngest son's arm.

"Mom, chill." My son wasn't being disrespectful, he was merely exasperated.

I tried to relax. It was then that I realized the most terrifying thing: I had no control. I'd given it up to my teenage son. What was I thinking? I was now at the mercy of my child who, at the age of eighteen, thought he was invincible.

We made it home safe and sound and my three sons survived their teenage years. So did I, for that matter, but the driving lessons taught me that none of us are in control of our world except God, and nothing happens to us or our loved ones that He doesn't know about.

How remarkable that my sons learned to drive and I learned to trust the Lord that much more. ✻ AKB

Today's Prayer

Heavenly Father, remind us today that You command the sun and, tonight, the moon and stars just as You calmed the stormy sea more than two thousand years ago. Help us to trust You more and worry less. In Jesus' name, amen.

Guard Your Heart...

Keep your heart with all diligence, for out of it spring the issues of life.
PROVERBS 4:23 NKJV

few years ago, I started to notice an alarming trend in my circumstances. A morning trip to the gym was more like a stroll down a model's catwalk where interested parties scrutinized the goods, deciding whether or not I was worthy. Conversations, musings, and gripe sessions started to wear on my heart like sandpaper. On the way home from work, the car radio pumped out seductive rhythms with lyrics that made me, a grown woman never accused of being a prude, actually blush. And at the end of the day, television characters were swearing and scheming and sleeping with their best friends' spouses on every cable and network channel I flipped to.

By the time we climb into our beds at night, our hearts and minds have been exposed to so much friction that there is no alternative, if we're sensitive to the Holy Spirit: *This world wears on us.* We're like stones planted in a stream, and the rushing water of the most powerful current around us eventually changes us. That realization was the catalyst for me to make a commitment to the Lord that I would guard my heart more diligently.

Not a popular choice in a world gone slightly mad.

Have you ever noticed that the minute you take a stand, adversities immediately encroach? For instance, as soon as you say something like "I'm not going to eat any more chocolate this month!"...every square of chocolate in a sixty-mile radius suddenly races across your path. On a coworker's desk, at the bottom of your purse, in the kitchen cabinet behind the granola...*chocolate!*

That's the way it was after I decided to become more aware of what I took into my spirit. I set the car radio to contemporary Christian music and started reading at night instead of watching television, but it seemed like the war around me kicked it up a notch in response. I had to make a decision to continue in the battle, to *keep on keeping on* in the fight.

If, like me, you aren't the least bit interested in becoming one of a million other smooth stones lining the stream bed and would prefer instead to be the salt that seasons your environment, I encourage you to stand against the battle that rages on.

Despite the continuous barrage from the outside world in the form of well-meaning friends, media and general temptation, the effort to guard your heart is a worthy one. Start small. Raise your custom-made Harry Winston shield of faith, and get yourself fitted for your Jimmy Choos of peace. With the helmet of salvation and belt of truth already in place, you're far less likely to be washed away by the raging waters headed toward you. ✳ *SDB*

Today's Prayer

Father, thank You so much for the privilege of calling myself Your child. Help me today to season the world around me rather than the other way around. Show me opportunities to draw closer to You, and to maintain the textures You added when You created me. In Jesus' precious name I pray.

I Wanna Be Like George

Pray without ceasing.

1 Thessalonians 5:17 kjv

I saw the neatest thing while surfing TV channels in the wee hours of the morning...a quote from George Washington's prayer journal. Scatterbrained me scribbled a note so that, later, I'd remember to investigate the journals of the father of our country.

Well, the sun rose—and thanks to my typically crazy-busy morning, the note was quickly buried beneath my shopping list, my to-do list, bills to be paid, and reminders of phone calls to return. When at last I sat down to begin my workday, I asked God to lead my tasks and the order in which I should perform them.

I'm sure you aren't surprised to learn that He reminded me about Washington's prayer journals. Obediently, I logged on to the Internet and found dozens of sites dedicated to the man's *spiritual* life. Fascinated, I read the heartfelt pleas made daily by this busy, important man and had to ask myself: If George the general, president, and husband and father found time to sit down and write meaningful, heartfelt words to the Lord God every day, why couldn't I?

Join me, won't you, in today's prayer, quoted from George Washington's journal. ✽ *LL*

Today's Prayer

"Direct my thoughts, words, and work. Wash away my sins in the immaculate blood of the Lamb, and purge my heart by Thy Holy Spirit...that I may with more freedom of mind and liberty of will, serve Thee, the everlasting God...."

Elvis Has Left the Building

Then he said to me, "This is the curse that goes out over the face of the whole earth:
'Every thief shall be expelled,' according to this side of the scroll; and,
'Every perjurer shall be expelled,' according to that side of it."

ZECHARIAH 5:3 NKJV

Yesterday I went to everyone's favorite big-box store in search of bargains. With the economy like it is today, who can afford to pay full price for anything? As I entered and walked past the greeter, an ominous feeling flooded me. The store was packed with moms pushing shopping carts, tired folks riding electric carts, and an assortment of harried men looking for socks/T-shirts/cookies/candy/whatever. I took a quick glance at my list to see if I could justify postponing my shopping or taking it elsewhere. Nope. There were too many things we needed, and by shopping at this particular store, the savings were substantial enough to plow forward.

I started in the book section, made my way over to the health-and-beauty aisle, and wound up in the electronics department, where I loaded my cart with paper and printer ink. As I turned the corner and headed toward the dairy aisle, I spotted a middle-aged woman dropping CDs from the sale bin into her tote as she nervously glanced around. The instant our gazes met, she knew I was on to her. She quickly turned and scurried off. My heart sank as I thought about my dilemma. The woman was clearly in the process of stealing merchandise, but I didn't have a lot of time because of an impending deadline. If I said something to management, I'd be detained, and there was no way I'd get out of the store in a timely manner. However, if I kept this little secret, I was pretty sure that would make me an accessory to the crime. As uncomfortable as it was, I knew what I needed to do. I'd ask the woman if she needed help buying her CDs. Maybe that would embarrass her enough to make her put them back. Okay, probably not, but it was worth a try.

Shoving my nearly empty cart in the direction the woman had gone, I had to dodge other shoppers. Then, suddenly, I saw the woman sobbing as she stood next to the store employee who'd apprehended her. I should have had more faith in the store security cameras.

After I paid, loaded up my car with the bargains, and headed home, I let out a deep sigh as I thought about that woman who was willing to take the risk of stealing store merchandise—clearly not necessary items. Was she a kleptomaniac? Or did she have a thing for Elvis? Whatever the case, she felt entitled to help herself to stuff that didn't belong to her. Now what would happen to her? Probably not much for a few CDs, but still...

I was relieved that someone else had confronted this woman before I spoke to her, because I really didn't want to pay for her CDs. What should we do when we see someone in the act of doing something wrong? Is it up to us to confront that person or turn her in? Either decision is difficult, no matter what. I prayed for her when I got home, and I'll continue to pray for her—that the Lord will rescue her from this sin. At the same time, I need to remember that my own sin nature is no better—that when I covet something I have no business having, I'm as bad as a thief. Even if it is just an Elvis CD. ✳ DM

Today's Prayer

Dear Lord, heavenly Father, I pray for Your righteous justice for this woman and for everyone, because we're all sinners. Bring us discernment and judgment as we go through each day, and help us to make the right decisions. In Your holy name, amen.

When a DIL Goes AWOL

Hatred stirs up strife, but love covers all sins.
PROVERBS 10:12 NKJV

I have three sons. And when they got married I didn't think of myself as losing my precious "little boys," just gaining sweet, beautiful daughters.

Daughters. *At last* I wasn't outnumbered in a house full of males. I had someone to go shopping with while the Green Bay Packers played football on Sunday afternoons.

I felt particularly close to one DIL (daughter-in-law). I had led her to Christ before she and my son were married, and we had an amazing way of thinking along the same lines about various issues and situations. We could talk for hours. Once, when they stopped by to drop off something on their way to a dinner engagement, my son wouldn't even let my DIL get out of their SUV. He knew all too well that she and I would start gabbing and they'd never get to where they were going on time. I remember telling her that if I had ever had a daughter, it'd be her. She, in turn, sent me cards and bought me little treasures, many of which touted the joys of the mother/daughter relationship. She called me, sent emails, and made sure my son didn't forget Mother's Day.

So when I learned she'd filed for divorce, my heart broke.

For months I'd had inklings that something was amiss between my DIL and my son. I'd tried approaching him, asking questions, but he didn't appreciate what he perceived as my meddling. I conversed with my DIL and she revealed a few things; however, none seemed serious enough to end their five-year marriage. I backed off, not wanting to be that proverbial busybody MIL (mother-in-law).

Later I learned the truth; my DIL had met another guy and wanted to be with him.

"What about trust, honor, and commitment?" I wanted to shout at her. As she was in the military, I thought she reverenced those traits. Obviously she didn't. I had been wrong to assume otherwise. She didn't want to be my son's wife and part of our family anymore.

So much for having a daughter.

"You must hate her," a coworker remarked when I mentioned my son's pending divorce.

To my shame, I confessed that maybe I did hate her just a little bit—at first. But then God showed me that if you really love someone, you love that person forever, unconditionally...and I truly love my DIL.

Even now.

Months later, she and I met for lunch, facing each other for the first time since she'd filed for divorce. I greeted her with a hug—and before any words were spoken, my DIL sobbed and sobbed. I sensed the hurt that ran so deep within her. I wished she'd have let God heal her emotional wounds instead of turning to a new boyfriend who wouldn't ever meet that need.

When, at last, we finally talked, I was able to share my heart in a loving way. I said I didn't approve of her behavior, the adultery, but that I still loved her. She admitted that she thought I'd hate her. I assured her that I didn't. After all, what could hate accomplish when love conquers all? ✳ AKB

Today's Prayer

Lord, there are people in our lives who have hurt us and/or hurt the ones we deeply love. Help us to understand that we don't have to accept their wrongdoings as right, but we must forgive the person who committed the wrongdoing. Once we forgive them, Your peace that passes all understanding will fill our hearts and minds. Grant us this peace. We pray this in Jesus' name, amen.

Oops! Wrong Building!

You will show me the path of life;
in Your presence is fullness of joy;
at Your right hand are pleasures forevermore.

PSALM 16:11 NKJV

My mom was the youngest of eight children, and each of her siblings was very different from the others, but my special favorite was Aunt Mary. She was a perfect combination of Mrs. C. from *Happy Days* and Edith Bunker from *All in the Family*—a pure mixture of heart and truth. Just when you thought she might actually be off her rocker, Aunt Mary would come up with something that was pure gold.

I spent time with her over the summer whenever I could. She lived in a tiny town called Barberton where the most exciting thing we ever did was meet a couple of my aunts for lunch and shop for yarn at the Five-and-Dime afterward or take a drive into the country to buy produce for dinner from a roadside stand. I would never admit it to anyone at the time, but I loved those vacations in Barberton.

One particularly hot summer, I visited Aunt Mary for a week, when I was absolutely heartbroken over a boy back home. He'd asked one of my best friends to the autumn dance instead of me, and I felt as if my teenage life was over.

"I did everything I could to make him like me," I declared. "I wore my hair the way he liked it; I had him over for swimming dates and barbecues. I even let him beat me at Monopoly! I just can't understand what I did wrong."

I'll never forget that moment.

Aunt Mary was drying dishes, and she turned around, leaned against the sink, and sighed.

"You just leaned your ladder against the wrong building," she said.

That was the kind of thing she would often say. No hint about what it meant, but it was delivered with such an expression of assurance that you just knew something was there. Somewhere.

"I was at the market," she explained, "and I saw a magazine at the checkout with a big headline on it reading, 'So busy climbing the corporate ladder that you haven't realized your ladder is up against the wrong building?'"

Hmm...I'm sorry. What?

"That's you," she stated. "You were so busy trying to get a boyfriend, you didn't stop to think that you might be chasing after the wrong boy."

And there it was. Pure gold.

More than four decades have passed since that summer with Aunt Mary, but I can remember the moment like it was yesterday. I've leaned my ladder against a lot of wrong buildings in my life, but her words often act as the ringing bell that causes me to step back and re-evaluate.
* *SDB*

Today's Prayer

I praise Your holy name, Lord Jesus. And I pray that You will help me today to remember that You have a plan for me and that there is a path all cleared and ready for me to follow. In Your precious name I pray, amen.

Be Nice (Especially When It's Tough)!

Add to your faith...patience; and to patience godliness; and to godliness brotherly kindness....

2 PETER 1:5–7 KJV

esterday, as I stood in the grocery store checkout line, I grew a little flustered while rummaging in my purse for money and my "reduce the price" card. (Maybe you have one of those bottomless pit satchels that allows you to carry everything but the kitchen sink, too....) In my overzealousness to dig for my wallet, my address book fell out and slid under the magazine rack.

Well, imagine my surprise when the gentleman behind me got onto his hands and knees on my behalf! He got up, dusted off his trousers *and* the mini phone book, and winked. "There you go, little lady," he said, smiling. My heartfelt "Thank you" hardly seemed sufficient, but what more could I do...or say?

The nice man and I chatted as my purchases rolled by on the black conveyor belt: The weatherman predicted rain tonight; weren't those tabloid headlines hilarious; he hoped the tickle in his throat wouldn't become the full-blown flu that had laid his wife low all week....

Something inching down the conveyor belt—a two-for-one package of an effervescent product that promised to nip germs in the bud—caught my eye. While he distractedly searched his pocket for a credit card, I paid for it, separated the two products, and handed one to him.

The poor guy looked as shocked as I'd felt when he hit the floor to retrieve my address book. Isn't it a shame that small acts of kindness like that aren't a routine part of everyone's days!

Driving home, I remembered the story of the little girl who walked along the seashore after high tide and found a dozen starfish on the sand. Bending down, she picked one up as a man passing by said, "You realize, don't you, that it's impossible to save them all." The little girl tossed the starfish into the water. "Maybe," she replied, "but at least I saved *that* one."

As I put away my groceries, I turned on the small black-and-white TV in my kitchen and saw what has become my all-time favorite commercial: A man picks up an empty soda bottle on the ground at a county fair and tosses it into a trash can; a woman on the Ferris wheel, who'd witnessed this good citizen's behavior, later helps an elderly gentleman climb the stairs; a mom sees her act of kindness and returns photos forgotten by a young couple on a carnival ride...and on and on.

These seemingly insignificant displays of good citizenship, of human compassion, of *Christianity,* make us all feel a little better about ourselves, our lives, and the world at large. And isn't it wonderful that those feelings are contagious!

We needn't be "out and about" to participate in such behavior. We could, instead, call a relative who's trying to survive the anniversary of a loved one's passing. Or email a friend to say happy birthday. Rake leaves or shovel snow for an elderly neighbor. Don't ask permission or make an announcement—just do it! So go ahead...infect someone in *your* world with kindness today! ✳ *LL*

Today's Prayer

Lord above, open my eyes to the needs of others and blind me to my own. Enhance my hearing so I'll notice when someone needs a word of encouragement or compassion. Thank You, Father, for emboldening my heart so I'll have the courage to act each time I encounter a person in need of kindness. Amen.

Are We There Yet?

So you may walk in the way of goodness,
and keep to the paths of righteousness.

PROVERBS 2:20 NKJV

Every person who has ever traveled with a child has heard, "Are we there yet?" And after the first dozen or so times, the answer is almost always preceded by a sigh and what feels like a recorded answer: "Not yet. Why don't you take a nap, so the time will go by faster?"

My children were always excited to go anywhere that involved packing their little purple "I love Grandma" suitcases and loading up the car with snacks and coloring books. They were generally pretty good for the first hour or so. However, it didn't take long before we started hearing noise from the backseat—little voices whining, "Are we there yet?" "How much longer?" "I'm tired," "Tell Daddy to drive faster," or "Why is it taking so long, Mommy? Are we lost?"

No, we weren't there; it would be another four, six, or eight hours. I often said, "Daddy can't drive faster because he's already going the speed limit" and "No, we're not lost."

Since most of our trips were to one of the grandparents' houses or our favorite beach in Florida, we knew the way. As long as we stayed on the familiar roads, there was no problem in getting there. We knew that if we took a detour, we might get lost, so we rarely did that.

Every destination has its own path—some extremely popular and others not so crowded. The times in my life that I've followed the enticements of the not-so-righteous target, I've quickly learned that the fun is short-lived. After the party was over and everyone was gone, a sad, often listless feeling overwhelmed me. The popular path may look shiny and pretty, but beneath the very thin surface, I've discovered slippery mud and quicksand.

Sometimes when things get rough, I wonder why I'm "not there yet." Then there are times when I'm offered little tidbits and signs that help to keep me focused on Him. Getting there is going to be amazing, but the journey is necessary and should be appreciated.

Fortunately for all sinners, God is ready to welcome us as the best earthly father should welcome his child. Are we there yet? Not yet, but I know that my journey down this solid path is much more rewarding than any created by my sinful nature. ✳ DM

Today's Prayer

Dear Lord, thank You for always welcoming me back after I stray.
I pray that You'll be with me as I try to stay focused on Your Word,
regardless of how tempting it is to stray. Amen.

Husband for Sale—Cheap!

Wives, submit to your own husbands, as to the Lord.
For the husband is head of the wife, as also Christ is head of the church;
and He is the Savior of the body. Therefore, just as the church is subject to Christ,
so let the wives be to their own husbands in everything.

EPHESIANS 5:22–24 NKJV

I love my husband. He's a great guy. He tries very hard to make me happy—and he's usually successful. I'm basically a joyful woman.

But there are times when I'd like to sell off my beloved to the highest bidder. Make that *any* bidder! It's those frustrating times when he won't share his thoughts with me and decisions have to be made; I need to know what he's thinking! It's those aggravating moments when I try to tell him about a personal crisis and he rolls his eyes like I've just uttered the stupidest thing in the world.

Okay, sure, he's put up with a lot from me. I like to shop. But he likes to watch football, basketball, and baseball on TV (throw NASCAR into that mix, too). Yeah, I suppose my habit is more expensive. However, I do have a job outside the home and contribute to our family's income. But it's also true that I write books, short stories, and devotions (an all-consuming ministry) when I could be spending time with him—but if he doesn't talk anyhow, what's the point? Oh, and I can't forget that for the first twenty-five years of our marriage, my husband suffered through my PMS (that's "post" and "pre"). But I gave him three wonderful, healthy sons—and he didn't have to do anything but stand there and watch me push and strain as our boys entered the world. What's more, he snored right through the 2 a.m. feedings—make that the 2, 4, and 6 a.m. feedings!

But over the years, he's proved himself faithful. There have been no other women in his life. (I think I'm all he can handle.) He doesn't do drugs, drink, smoke, or chew. He makes my lunch for me before I leave for work. He habitually checks my minivan's oil and the air pressure in its tires. He makes sure my vehicle is washed. He does the laundry (I can't remember the last time I used the washing machine), and he loads and unloads the dishwasher. He loves me and would do anything for me if he thought it would make me happy. Most of all, he loves the Lord Jesus Christ.

Can a woman really ask for anything more? Sure she can!

We're never truly satisfied, are we? That's human nature. The flesh. And the flesh wars against the Spirit of God, tugging, pulling, and causing us to see all the negative things in our spouses instead of focusing on the positive.

It's a constant battle, but our Lord is a forgiving God (1 John 1:9). He's also a God who has His hands firmly gripping the steering wheel of life. All we have to do is plant ourselves in the passenger seat and let Him take us where He will.

As for my husband—all bids are off, girls. I guess I'll keep him.

✱ AKB

Today's Prayer

Lord, forgive me for any resentment I might feel today toward my husband, and help me be respectful to him—just as I would toward You. Help me to remember that my husband is only human but that You are a wonder-working God who can and will sustain my marriage and increase my love for my husband. I ask this in Jesus' name, amen.

Ewww!

To console those who mourn in Zion,
to give them beauty for ashes, the oil of joy for mourning,
the garment of praise for the spirit of heaviness;
that they may be called trees of righteousness,
the planting of the LORD, that He may be glorified.

ISAIAH 61:3 NKJV

I am not much of a cook. I never have been. Bake some cookies or mix up a cake? I'm your girl. But the fine art of planning and executing a healthy, satisfying meal has traditionally been left to better women (and men, in some cases) than me.

For example, whenever I was hungry for yams, I went to the store, bought a can of them, and heated them up on the stove. So imagine my surprise when a friend invited me to dinner at her house and I saw her produce this huge, ugly, kidney-shaped thing out of the crisper in her refrigerator.

"What is that?" I asked her, and she stared at me as if my hair had caught on fire.

"What do you mean?" she asked.

"That. What is it?"

"It's a yam."

Interesting how something so ugly and misshapen could end up to be the beautiful dish she set out on the table an hour later. Peeled, cubed, and baked until soft with butter and brown sugar, that ugly yam had become appealing and delicious.

It occurred to me recently—I'm like that yam. Misshapen, to be sure; I'm no Jennifer Aniston! But what I have in common with that yam is *potential*.

On the occasions that I've suffered a devastating loss, even though at times I couldn't see it, there was recovery ahead. I would go on to live again, to smile, even to laugh. When I didn't think I had a song left in my heart, somehow I was able to hear the soft hum in the distance, the promise of music on my horizon.

The more often we experience His willingness to turn our mourning into joy and our ashes into something beautiful, the easier it is the next time to believe that we will survive. Like a muscle we've begun to exercise, our faith in what God will do in our lives is strengthened with its use.

I haven't bought a can of yams in years now. I love buying an ugly old yam and seeing if I can turn its "ashes" to something beautiful. Preferably with brown sugar! ✳ *SDB*

Today's Prayer

I am so humbled by Your ability to not only understand my deepest grief and concern but also to give me joy in place of mourning. You have turned my ashes into something beautiful by Your love. Help me today to bring joy and beauty into the lives around me and to display Your love through my every word and deed. In Your holy name I pray, amen.

To Do or Not to Do Is a Pretty Stupid Question

A man's heart deviseth his way:
but the LORD directeth his steps.

PROVERBS 16:9 KJV

As I sat scribbling my to-do list this morning, I was reminded of an ancient adage that goes something like, "Man plans while God laughs." It's times like these when I sense God whispering, "Loree, what is your hurry?"

Since I write (mostly) fiction for a living, it won't surprise you that on days like those, I imagine this conversation between God and me:

"What will happen if you don't scrub the kitchen floor or make the beds? Who would notice if the carpets aren't vacuumed or the end tables don't sparkle? Would anyone care if a few weeds sprout among the roses or fallen leaves collect on the welcome mat? And who'd point out that your ironing basket was full...or empty?"

"Well, for starters, my mother-in-law, that's who! And then there's my sister, and—"

"But I made your days to last twenty-four hours and not a moment more. How do you want to spend those hours? Ticking items off that to-do list of yours? Or setting aside time and energy to guarantee that you'll listen, really listen, to the cares of your hard-working husband at the end of the day?"

And my sweet daughters and grandkids, too, I thought. "But...but what will people think if they drop by and find dust bunnies on the hardwood or dishes in the sink?"

"They'll think you value the people who share your life more than those who might judge you 'less than perfect' if a few chores go undone."

(Now, really, how's a hard-workin' gal like me—who clocks sixty hours a week of housework, yard work, and *work*-work—supposed to react to that?)

And because *of course* He can hear my thoughts, He said, "By admitting that while hard work is a good thing, it can be addictive...."

"Hmm...is that why You inspired me to choose 'Good enough never is' and 'Do or do not; there *is* no try' as my life mottos?"

"Loree, my hardheaded daughter, put down your pen and pick up my Word. Five minutes there will change your mind and your thoughts—"

"—and ensure I'll smile, even if my mother-in-law shows up unexpectedly!" ❋ ℒℒ

Today's Prayer

O Lord, when I lay my weary head upon my pillow each night, I can't help but thank You for the lessons You so gently taught me throughout the day. Keep reminding me, sweet Jesus, what's truly important in life...and help me to erase what isn't from my to-do lists! Amen.

It Is What It Is

And the Word became flesh and dwelt among us, and we beheld His glory,
the glory as of the only begotten of the Father, full of grace and truth.
JOHN 1:14 NKJV

"What do you think Elizabeth Barrett Browning really thought about her husband?" my college poetry professor asked.

I tentatively lifted my hand. "When she said, 'How do I love thee, let me count the ways,' she meant she loved her husband."

"Look for the symbolism," he argued. "Was she starved for affection? Was she looking for affirmation of who she was as a woman? Did she have a secret? What was really going on with her?"

I disagreed with his theory that if poets wanted to tell it like it was, they'd do it in prose.

Sometimes it is what it is. I know that many poets use symbolism, metaphors, and irony to express themselves. However, I like to think that some verse is straightforward and honest.

It's like Christ's love for us. Yes, there are some poetic devices in the Bible, but there's never any doubt that His love for us is true. We don't have to guess or figure out what He means when He tells us He loves us. His Word is truth. I wanted to believe that my favorite romantic poetry was written about true love. Yet it's nothing like the most amazing and powerful love Christ has for us. ✳ DM

Today's Prayer

Your love for us, Jesus, is the best example we can follow.
I know I can't be perfect, but never let me forget what You did for all sinners.
You showed Your unconditional love in the most selfless way. Amen.

Addicted to...Fear?

...for the battle is the LORD's...

1 SAMUEL 17:47 NKJV

I'm watching the news. The anchorman is talking about tough economic times ahead. He refers to them as "an economic tsunami" that wipes out everyone. He predicts unemployment rates plummeting to lows not seen since 1945. I imagine a scene out of the novel *The Grapes of Wrath*. Would it really come to that?

Lifting the remote, I mute the TV. Next I pick up the phone and call my brother, a successful businessman. "What do you think, John?" I ask.

He replies with practical money-saving tips, but my fears aren't assuaged. I worry. I fret. My stomach hurts. My temples begin to throb.

Then I hear God's voice: "Be still, and know that I am God" (Psalm 46:10 NKJV). " 'Therefore I say to you, do not worry...which of you by worrying can add one cubit to his stature?' " (Luke 12:22–25 NKJV).

"Lord, I believe Your Word is true," I say, "but what if Dan's business fails? What if I lose my job? What if—"

" 'Do not fear...for it is your Father's good pleasure to give you the kingdom' " (Luke 12:32 NKJV).

The kingdom. So even if I lose every earthly possession, I'll still have a mansion in heaven awaiting me.

The truth sinks in. "Thank You, Jesus." My emotions begin to settle. I reach for the remote control so I can finish watching the television show. What other speculations would they make about these tumultuous times ahead?

Then I wonder: Am I addicted to fear? Didn't God just tell me not to worry?

I want to be informed about current events and yet I fret over that which I have no control. Does that make sense? Not hardly! Sure, I vote,

I write to my congressmen and senators about issues that are important to me, but the end result belongs to God. No situation rocks Him off His heavenly throne. After all, like David said before he killed the giant Goliath, "The battle is the Lord's." And guess what? God is always victorious!

I turn off the TV and decide to leave my worries for the future there—in God's most capable hands. ✳ AKB

Today's Prayer

Dear Lord, I believe; please help my unbelief at times when I feel scared about situations around me. Take away my worry and give me Your peace. You're the same God today who moved mountains and parted seas thousands of years ago. I put my wholehearted trust for my future in You. In Christ's name, amen.

Reality Does Bite!

*May the LORD answer you in the day of trouble; may the name of the God of Jacob
defend you; may He send you help from the sanctuary,
and strengthen you out of Zion; may He remember all your offerings,
and accept your burnt sacrifice. Selah. May He grant you
according to your heart's desire, and fulfill all your purpose.*

PSALM 20:1–4 NKJV

Some days take a real nip at your joy, don't they?

I always try to start my mornings with a little bit of Jesus—maybe a few minutes reading the Word or having a nice chat with Him while I'm putting on my makeup. And then each day, I walk out the door with the same words on my lips: "This is the day the Lord has made. I will rejoice and be glad in it!"

And I mean it, too. I'm determined. After all, my God has given me a pretty great life. I've survived cancer; I have great friends and a personable dog; and I'm surrounded with a lot of love. Best of all, despite the fact that I still work a "day job," I've finally begun to realize my dream of becoming a writer after a lifetime of hoping and trying. So when I walk out that door, proclaiming my intention to rejoice and be glad in the day the Lord has made just for me, I mean it. I'm going to do my job, try to bless someone along the way, and then head home for some time in front of the computer to work on my latest novel!

Ah, I'm such a very good planner. It's a gift, really.

Then comes the commute to work and the guy who cuts me off in traffic and makes me spill my coffee. This fun is almost always followed by my painstakingly organized calendar of duties getting shot with meeting requests, ringing phones, project emergencies, and coworkers who need a hand.

And so, by lunchtime, all those early morning thoughts of a nice dinner and a few writing hours at home after work begin to shred beneath the grinding, biting teeth of Reality.

I'm the type of person who can really be thrown off track by a few days like that in a row. Things start to back up on me, my calendar becomes a bit of a joke, and I find myself missing the breathtaking view of the forest for all the trees standing tall in front of me. In fact, I am often overwhelmed by those tall trees, and my methodical plans and godly purpose end up scattered and broken, roadkill on the shoulder of the highway that is my life.

I once had a friend ask me, "When is my life going to calm down?"

I had a moment of sheer clarity when I smiled and said, "It's not."

The truth is that this is the stuff life is made of. Interruptions and challenges, obstacles to overcome and mountains to climb: It all acts like iron against iron to grow us stronger throughout our lives. The best we can do is bounce back every now and then, remind ourselves what's most important, and take a deep breath and let it out slowly before we head out the door with words of assurance on our lips once again:

"This is the day the Lord has made. I will rejoice and be glad in it!"

✳ *SDB*

Today's Prayer

Father, thank You for holding my life in the palm of Your hand.
Help me today to remember that, no matter what happens, You and I are
in it together—and that You're leading me toward fulfilling my true purpose.
In Jesus' name I pray, amen.

Enough Already!

*But my God shall supply all your need
according to his riches in glory by Christ Jesus.*

PHILIPPIANS 4:19 KJV

I visited a friend's new house today and happily joined the tour of oohing and ahhing partygoers. Some drooled over Italian marble floors; others wished aloud for their very own room-sized closets, big-as-a-boat spa tubs, or state-of-the-art media centers.

I like to think I'm more practical than that. The objects of my desire nestled quietly in her expansive laundry room. *Whoa,* I thought, gawking at her pearly blue front-load washer and dryer, *think what quick work I could make of dirty clothes mountains if I had those! If I earn a few extra dollars here, gave a little less of myself there, maybe—*

Then the Lord reminded me of the prior weekend, when I'd babysat my six-year-old "grandtwins" and we'd watched some cartoons and children's movies on TV. Dozens of advertisements had hit their target audience and inspired the intended "I want that!" responses. "But you already have three talking Elmos!" and "You don't even play the piano you have!" I was quick to point out.

And in a flash of insight, I realized that what I and my friend's other guests had oohed about during our house tour and the things we'd ahhed about while watching made-for-grownups commercials for gadget-laden cars, high-def TVs, and computers capable of controlling the lights while balancing the checkbook and sending messages to friends from Toledo to Timbuktu—that was the same thing!

Constant exposure to such products and materials just tweaks our desire to acquire more, bigger, better. Almost from the moment we set our greedy, envious eyes on Things We Don't Yet Have, we set about devising ways to replace the Just Fine devices humming in our laundry rooms, making music in our parlors, and shining in our garages.

As I prayed about this, the Lord also reminded me of all those times when my mom—flustered by her kids' never-ending need for more—shouted, "Enough, already!" I wonder if our Father ever feels like bellowing a similar line at His children....

He's blessed us so richly, with so many gifts, that maybe in being surrounded by such surplus, we overlook what—and who—is truly important.

So I hope you won't think I've gone completely nuts when you see me at the mall shouting "Enough, already!" at my own reflection in store windows! ✳ *LL*

Today's Prayer

I'm on my knees, Lord, humbly asking forgiveness for any display
of want or greed I may have exhibited, however great or small.
Keep me ever-aware of the many wonderful gifts You've showered
upon me, and remind me—often—how truly fortunate I am.
Thank You, Father, for loving me despite my flaws!

Confessions of a Cookie-Cutter Christian

Let your eyes look straight ahead, and your eyelids look right before you.
PROVERBS 4:25 NKJV

*D*o you ever feel like you're walking in your sleep most of the time? I do.

I wake up every morning, turn on the computer, start the coffee, get the newspaper—and this is how my day begins. As I accomplish each task on my to-do list, I check it off—and then it's time for dinner. After the dishes are done I complete the rest of my daily routine—and then it's time for bed. On Sundays I get up, shower, get dressed for church, sit through the service, smile at folks as I walk out, and drive home to get ready for the workweek. How exciting, right? Um...not. More like bor–ing!

Sometimes it's so mundane, it all seems pointless. I feel like a cookie-cutter Christian. Everything is so repetitive that I don't bother to think about my actions. I'm easily distracted when I go through the repetitive motions of everyday life. Unfortunately, many of the world's most interesting distractions take my eyes off God.

By allowing myself to fall into the rut of living a cookie-cutter life, I'm not fulfilling my goal of walking in His light every single second of every single day. My daily schedule has taken over, and I'm not using the potential He gave me. Although not obviously evil, my attitude isn't right with God.

So what should I do? Find excitement for the sake of shaking things up? Or continue to go through life with the same routine until Jesus calls me home? Neither. I think I need to adjust my mind-set and attitude... and my routine. I should find more opportunities to serve Him and to reflect on His Word.

Rather than look at my tasks as boring and mundane, I should do them with joy while I focus on the light of His Word. Before I even get out of bed, I can read a single scripture verse to give me focus for my day. I think I might even add a few God-pleasing and interesting things to my to-do list to keep myself motivated. Not only will it help me walk in His path, but it will prevent me from straying into areas that I know aren't right for me. Varying the routine is fine as long as the purpose is to bring glory to God through Christ. ✳ *DM*

Today's Prayer

As I go through my day, Lord, keep me focused on You. Give me the spirit
of joy throughout my day, regardless of how routine my tasks are.
Don't let me forget that my ultimate goal is to draw closer to You—
and that's more exciting than anything the world can provide. Amen.

A Friend Is a Friend Is a Friend... Then Again, Maybe Not!

"Blessed are those who are persecuted for righteousness' sake, for theirs is the kingdom of heaven."

MATTHEW 5:10 NKJV

My husband, Daniel, was an alcoholic. He's not anymore. He's not even a "recovering alcoholic." Rather, he's a forgiven alcoholic, and he's been sober for some sixteen years. But it wasn't like God waved a magic wand and suddenly things were wonderful. Daniel and I were met with a succession of trials, but the Lord saw us through.

One Sunday night a special speaker came to our church and delivered an impromptu message on the sin of alcoholism. This speaker had planned to talk about something else that night; however, our local newspaper had run a story in its Sunday edition about how Wisconsin is in the top ranks for being home to the most alcoholics in the United States. After all, we are basically the beer capital of the world.

The speaker's message really touched my husband; he realized he didn't have to rehash all the ugliness of his past or go through years of counseling in order to quit drinking. He just had to repent and turn from it, embrace God's goodness, and accept God's healing.

That's the first step. Next came telling our friends and family members that we had both quit drinking.

Now you'd think people would be happy when an alcoholic says, "I'm done drinking and hurting my family. I'm starting a whole new life." But, incredibly, the opposite is often true. Some of our family members actually tried to sabotage Daniel's resolution. Our close friends stopped inviting us to their homes and to parties. It broke my heart to realize that my friends weren't true friends; they'd merely been drinking buddies. However, we found support at our local church. We made new friends—good friends. We still had fun. In fact, we've had more fun because we're not sick and hungover the next day! We might have lost a lot at first, but God replaced everything we lost and added more.

Stepping out into the Light takes a lot of courage. Be prepared for the backlash. Steady yourself with God's Word—and then enjoy the insurmountable blessings that follow! ✱ AKB

Today's Prayer

Lord God, You alone are able to remove any addictions from our lives.
Just say the words and we will be healed. It's as simple as that...and yet
what follows might prove to be the hardest days of our lives. Help us to let go
of dysfunctional relationships and accept new and healthy ones.
Help us stay in Your Light so we never experience the darkness again!
In Christ's name we ask, amen.

The Value of Time

The LORD God is my strength;
He will make my feet like deer's feet,
and He will make me walk on my high hills.

HABAKKUK 3:19 NKJV

*B*ack in college, Maureen was one of my closest friends. When I discovered her in the parking lot, slumped over the wheel of her car and crying, I opened the door and climbed in beside her.

"What did he do?"

Blaming her on-again, off-again boyfriend, Craig, was always the first response.

"It's not Craig," she told me. "It's my parents."

A week before Thanksgiving break, Maureen's parents had sent her a gift certificate to an elegant local restaurant. It seemed they had decided to go away on a cruise over the holiday, and they'd sent her a certificate to have Thanksgiving dinner on them. Alone.

Maureen came from a dairy farm dynasty. Eggs, milk, that kind of thing. Okay, so calling it a *dynasty* might not be accurate, but, all things being relative, my middle-class upbringing would likely appear as a scene out of *Oliver Twist*, in comparison. Despite that, I couldn't see my friend eating turkey at a table for one, so I invited her to come home with me.

If there is one thing memorable about my family, it's that there was always room at our table for a few more. If there were more than six of us eating at a given time, well, we just moved in a chair or two from the kitchen. So what if the plates didn't match or the drinking glasses had yellow sunflowers etched on some and American flags on others. Our dining room table was the gathering place, a melting pot of friends, family, and assorted strays.

The turkey was perfect, even if there was too much sage in the stuffing. My mom knew how to lay out a spread! There was a variety of vegetables, a dozen different starches, and desserts that crowded the large table in the kitchen. Mom lit bright blue candles that didn't match anything, and our neighbor's grandson spilled milk from one end of the dining room table to the other.

When I drove Maureen back to campus that night, I half expected her to say something like, "That was, uh, very special. Thanks."

Instead, the minute we got into my car, she burst into tears.

"I know. The stuffing was heartbreaking," I said.

"What a beautiful family you have," she exclaimed. "Thank you so much for letting me be part of your holiday."

We didn't say much more in the car that night, but I've never forgotten my moment of realization. Maureen didn't care about the menu for the Thanksgiving meal. She cared about being part of something. And now that I'm grown and my parents are gone, I often feel as if I'm walking in Maureen's shoes—grateful when friends open up their homes, allowing me to share in their celebrations, and happy to be a part of something again. ✳ *SDB*

Today's Prayer

Lord, thank You for not just giving me strength; thank You for being my strength. My faith in You makes me part of something so much larger than myself, and I pray that You will help me to be a conduit of Your grace and love in the lives of everyone I meet. In Jesus' name I pray. Amen.

Saving Cash

But the fruit of the Spirit
is love, joy, peace, longsuffering
gentleness, goodness, faith....
GALATIANS 5:22 KJV

My husband and I adopted a dog seven years ago. Not a cute little sit-in-your-lap, follow-at-your-heels puppy, but a ninety-pound, drooling, lumbering, clumsy beast that we call Cash.

To say that his former owner mistreated him would be the proverbial understatement of the year. Thanks to regular beatings and general neglect, Cash and his littermates endured broken bones that healed on their own, infections that went untreated, and conditions like heartworm and Lyme disease that were ignored. They lived outside, regardless of the weather, with just enough food and barely enough water to sustain them. When neighbors complained about the nonstop whimpering and whining coming from the owner's property, he was forced to choose: Give up the dogs or face fines and jail time.

Enter Larry and Loree, who, months earlier, buried the pet cat that had lived with them for nearly nineteen years. It took a few months, but Cash helped us to learn that "having a cat" and "being owned by a dog" are vastly different things!

He started out behaving like he was afraid of just about everything—like flashlights (one tool used by his former owner to torture him), thunderstorms, cameras, 99 percent of the men who visited us, and bugs...especially those with wings. Slowly his skittish behavior disappeared and was replaced by doggy games like "Scare the Delivery Boy!" and "Terrify the Meter Reader!"

I'm always amazed at how this enormous lumbering beast who, with a mere look, can flatten a burly six-foot-tall repairman against a wall but becomes a meek little lamb when children are around. Newborns, toddlers, kindergarteners...he loves them all, and he happily greets each with a gentle (if not wet-and-sloppy) kiss.

He's a lesson in opposites, this magazine-shredding, hair-shedding, muddy-paw-print-making dog of ours. Instead of the once-abused/now-abusive mutt people warned us he might become, Cash is a shining example of what can happen when one is open to love, kindness, understanding, and compassion.

And he was more than open to ours!

If I could figure out how to get this Transformation Information from Cash to my two-legged peers, wouldn't the world would be a happier place!

So the real question is—did we save Cash, or did *he* save us? ✳ *LL*

Today's Prayer

Beloved Lord, allow me to find ways every day to reach out to those who are hurting and frightened. Bless me with the strength of character and the words to comfort them, and give me an attitude that will let them know they are welcome and treasured. Amen.

Get Real, Cinderella

Or do you not know that your body is the temple of the Holy Spirit who is in you, whom you have from God, and you are not your own?

1 CORINTHIANS 6:19 NKJV

Some days I get out of bed feeling frumpy and ugly. I suspect hormones play a role in that, but seriously, no matter how hard I try, I can't seem to get rid of those ten or twenty pounds that keep me from wearing my favorite jeans.

Where is my fairy godmother? Did someone hijack her on her way to rescue me from thunder thighs, a flabby belly, and saggy boobs? I've watched all the style shows that demonstrate how to hide "problem areas," but what happens if my problem area is head to toe?

Why do men never worry about body image? My husband can stand in front of a mirror without a shirt and actually come away from it happy. There are days when I avoid mirrors or clean windows, no matter how far out of my way I have to go. For once, I'd like to be able to stand in front of a mirror, look at myself without being critical, and stop worrying about every single imperfection gawking back at me.

The female body is constantly being measured—either favorably or as an example of how not to be—throughout life. We're put on a pedestal, ogled, and discussed as though we're a commodity, which is all wrong. I know that, but I still often feel as if everyone belongs at the royal ball but me. Pick up any women's magazine and you'll see what I'm talking about.

As Christian women, our bodies no longer belong to us. Christ lives in us, so we should respect who we are without all the disturbing worldly messages tearing us down. Being of strong, moral character is much more attractive to believers in Christ than the sexual objects portrayed by Hollywood. No amount of plastic surgery, Botox, or collagen can

give us the inner beauty that glows from the love of Christ. Deep down we know what's important, and honey, the Cinderella story is nothing compared to the true love God showed us through His Son, Jesus Christ.
✳ DM

Today's Prayer

Keep me focused on what is pleasing to You, Lord. Your love is much deeper than anything portrayed by the media and much more real than the physical attributes shown as "perfect." Remind me to keep it real and to never lose sight of the true beauty of Your love. Amen.

Send in the Angels

But he himself went a day's journey into the wilderness, and came and sat down under a juniper tree; and he requested for himself that he might die, and said, "It is enough; now, O LORD, take my life, for I am not better than my fathers."

1 KINGS 19:4 NASB

Many years ago my son came home from kindergarten singing a little ditty that went something like this: "Nobody loves me. Everybody hates me. Let's just go eat worms."

It wasn't until years later that I saw how relevant those words might seem to someone with hopelessness.

A woman came to work in my department at the hospital. She felt totally lost among all the tasks she'd been assigned. She felt like others in the department weren't nice to her because she was new and didn't know what she was doing yet. No matter how hard she tried, it all seemed useless. She wanted to quit. But another coworker and I (both Christians) noticed what was happening, and we took her under our wings and coached her along.

To this day Deb (who is still working in that department, quite successfully) tells me that I was one of her "angels" during that time.

In the prophet Elijah's case, he had Queen Jezebel threatening to kill him. He got tired of running and fighting and wanted to give up. He wanted God to take his life because he felt he hadn't made any more difference to the Lord than the generations that had come before him. But in the next passage, the Bible tells us: "He lay down and slept under a juniper tree; and behold, there was an angel touching him, and he said to him, 'Arise, eat' " (1 Kings 19:5 NASB).

In other words, God's angel gave Elijah a little TLC when he needed it most.

This passage is a wonderful example of how God works in those hours when we feel like giving up on our jobs, our families, our friends—maybe even on life. He sends an angel, perhaps in the form of another one of God's children, to carry words of hope and encouragement—and maybe even chocolate chip cookies! (Better than eating worms, that's for sure!)

Who knows...maybe God will use you as an angel in disguise to bring His love and mercy to another hurting soul. ✳ AKB

Today's Prayer

Dear heavenly Father, thank You for Your love, grace, and mercy toward us. Help us to be sensitive to the needs of others, and use us as angels in disguise. Let others see Jesus in us today.
In His name, we ask, amen.

When Did He Get So Smart?

When You said, "Seek My face," my heart said to You,
"Your face, Lord, I will seek."

PSALM 27:8 NKJV

I was a "daddy's girl" when I was growing up. My six-foot-three-inch tough-guy Marine Corps–officer father was often putty in my hands. I knew just how to get around him.

So imagine my surprise when, at the age of sixteen, I helped my mom with dinner, washed the dishes afterward, and then presented my father's favorite (banana cream pie) for dessert...but I couldn't get him to agree to allow me to join my boyfriend's band on a national tour!

"You should have asked me before you went to all this trouble," he told me. "The answer would have been the same."

In that universal sixteen-year-old way, I was aghast! All his fatherly reasons why I wasn't going to be allowed to spend my summer touring the country with my boyfriend were pretty much lost on me. I wanted to go, and my mind was racing with ideas on how I could make that happen.

"You know," my dad said to me later that night, "someday you're going to ask me something and, after I answer, you're going to wonder to yourself, 'When did my old man get so smart?' "

"Well, this isn't that day," I replied dryly.

I know. I was a haughty teenager.

"So this is probably like spitting into the wind," he said from the doorway of my bedroom, "but I'm going to say it to you anyway. There is no price tag hanging on your well-being. There aren't enough chores you can do or pies you can make to buy an answer you want to hear when it's something that I feel is going to interfere with your safety."

It wasn't until years later that I realized how my dad had quickly discerned the motives behind my actions that day—and so many other days, too. He loved it when I helped around the house and made sure to be at the table with the family for dinner, and he was so appreciative when I went out of my way to do something I knew would please him. But the fact that I knew that and, typical of a teenager, used it to try to get something in return took all the flavor out of it for him.

My father didn't want anything from me except my love and respect. He wanted me to spend time with the family because they were important to me. He wanted me to "seek his face," not what he might be holding in his hand.

Honestly, I can't help wondering as I look back: *When did he get so smart?* ✽ *SDB*

Today's Prayer

Lord Jesus, I love You so much. And today I seek Your face...
and Your touch...and Your voice...and Your sweet presence.
There is nothing else more important this day than drawing closer
to my Creator. In Jesus' name, amen.

A "Work" in Progress

In all thy ways, acknowledge him, and he shall direct thy paths.

PROVERBS 3:6 KJV

A few weeks ago, I applied for the position of assistant editor for a local newspaper. But every time I prayed about this job, I was left with a feeling that I should just wait.

A few days after my interview, I ran into a former student who's a secretary at the publication. I understood why I'd been so unsettled when the woman went on to tell me about problems at her newspaper. Crazy things were going on over there, she admitted, with editors being axed, reporters quitting right and left, and morale at an all-time low. She had no idea what had caused all the unrest, but she concluded with a warning to expect a call from her boss about "my" job.

Then in today's mail was a fat envelope from one of the companies that publishes my novels, filled with letters from my readers. "I love your stories!" said one. "Please don't ever stop writing!" said another. I heard God's voice telling me that He speaks to my readers through the stories I write. "This is the gift I have given to you," He seemed to be saying, "to touch My children's hearts and stir their souls."

I went straight to the phone, withdrew my job application, and headed to my desk to work on my latest idea. He has made me a missionary with the books I write, delivering His Word to those in need. ✱ *LL*

Today's Prayer

Sweet Jesus, I thank You ever-so-humbly for guiding
every facet of my life. You steer me from paths where I don't belong
and onto those that You have chosen for me! Amen.

Zip It!

Therefore you are inexcusable, O man, whoever you are who judge,
for in whatever you judge another you condemn yourself;
for you who judge practice the same things.
But we know that the judgment of God is according to truth
against those who practice such things.
And do you think this, O man,
you who judge those practicing such things, and doing the same,
that you will escape the judgment of God?

ROMANS 2:1–3 NKJV

*D*id you hear about Connie Cubicle? I heard that she was written up because she spent all day surfing the Internet at the office."

"I heard that Mr. and Mrs. Rotten Neighbor were getting a divorce and she took off without the kids."

"Can you believe that Suzie Shortskirt came to work dressed like *that*?"

Or how about, "*My* kids would *never* do that"?

I can't even count the times I've looked at someone else and judged them when they 1) wore something too tight/too short/too gaudy, 2) let their kids throw temper tantrums in public, 3) did something unethical on the job, or 4) made a bad decision in a relationship. It's bad enough to judge these people in my own mind, but what makes it worse is when I tell someone what I'm thinking.

That's gossip.

No one wants to think of themselves as a gossip, but anytime we talk about someone else with an ounce of judgment, that's exactly what it is. Now, my question is, who is so perfect that they're above being judged?

Not me, that's for sure.

How about when someone tells you they know something no one else knows about the person on the other side of the office wall, and they're dying to share it with you? Whenever I hear this, I mentally rub my hands together, round my shoulders like a raccoon ready to dive into a Dumpster, and prepare myself for some juicy tidbits that'll make me feel superior.

That's gossip, too.

Even when we aren't the ones spreading the information, we're just as guilty of gossip when we listen to it because we're providing the opportunity for those who do the talking. It might make us feel good to be in-the-know for a little while, but that feeling doesn't last long. After a day or two, it plays on our minds and in our hearts, making us feel dirty and slimy—whether we're the ones spreading the gossip or the person on the receiving end.

It's just wrong, either way.

Every day, I need to focus on how I can help others rather than bring them down, no matter how much short-lived fun it is to talk about them. When someone says something judgmental about another person, I should try stopping the negativity and turning it around to see if there's something we can do to make things better. That's what God would want us to do. ✳ DM

Today's Prayer

Dear Lord, use me to lift other people when they're down. Help me to resist the temptation to squash them and damage their reputations. Give me the strength to stop ugly rumors and gossip. Put only positive words that are pleasing to You on my tongue. Amen.

Why Isn't My Faith Enough?

And He said to her,
"Daughter, your faith has made you well.
Go in peace, and be healed of your affliction."

MARK 5:34 NKJV

For years I prayed that God would heal me from my fibromyalgia. But instead of complete wellness, I developed other health issues, including small fiber neuropathy (SFN), something that preempts diabetes. I've changed my diet and now include exercise. I'm maintaining; however, there are still "down days" when I struggle with pain issues. It can get depressing sometimes.

So when I first heard the latter diagnosis leave my neurologist's mouth, I felt more than a little discouraged. I wondered why God didn't heal me.

My supervisor urged me to apply for a special program at my employer's occupational health department so if I was absent because of one of my chronic issues, I wouldn't lose my job. I filled out the paperwork and sent it to my MD. When I received the completed list from my physician, I stared at it in amazement. Eight chronic illnesses were listed.

"And you're working almost full-time?"

I looked up at the woman in Occ Health. I'm sure she normally wouldn't remark on an employee's personal information, but I knew her somewhat from coming into the office so many times. We had chatted here and there.

"That's amazing," she said. "And you write books, too? How do you manage it all? I mean, I know people with one or two illnesses on your list who are completely disabled. You've got eight."

"God's grace, I suppose."

"Then there really must be a God."

Now, I didn't know where this woman stood spiritually, but I realized in that moment that the Lord had just used my health issues to prove His sovereignty, love, and grace. He'd worked through me, and I wondered if that's why the Lord hadn't miraculously healed me—just like the apostle Paul who suffered with "infirmities" and learned that God's strength is made perfect in our weakness (2 Corinthians 12:9).

In her devotional book called *God of All Comfort*, Judy Gann writes: "God can remove our illnesses and change our circumstances in an instant—the moment they are no longer needed for His divine purposes. Until then, or until He takes us home, we can rest in the fact that our illnesses are part of His good purpose for our lives. God truly uses all things."

I slowly came to realize that there is purpose in my pain and it's not a question of my faith: It's a matter of God's will. ✳ *AKB*

Today's Prayer

Lord, thank You for sustaining us through sickness and in health.
Remind us that we can find joy in whatever physical state we're in.
We trust that You are using our health, be it good or poor, to Your glory.
We praise You for the unexpected miracles to come. In Jesus' name, amen.

God of All Comfort by Judy Gann was published by Living Ink Books, a division of AMG Publishers, in 2005. Selection taken from page 10.

A Promise Kept

Behold, the former things have come to pass,
and new things I declare;
before they spring forth I tell you of them.

ISAIAH 42:9 NKJV

The accident wasn't my fault. A black Toyota Camry flew between moving traffic and headed straight for me. In an effort to swerve out of his way, I slammed directly into the car beside mine. To make matters worse, that Camry was long gone by the time the police arrived.

"Were you on your cell phone?" the stern officer asked me. "What else would make you swerve out of the lane and into this other car? Don't you know how dangerous it can be to talk on your cell phone while driving?"

"I don't even own a cell phone!" I objected, and they looked at me as if my hair were on fire.

I could see the question in the officer's eyes: *What kind of American doesn't own a cell phone?* One like me at the time, but I didn't have the opportunity to tell him so.

"It wasn't her fault. She was forced off the road."

Relief flooded over me! This complete stranger had seen the accident happen, and he stepped forward to speak up on my behalf. And when the insurance company of the other driver summoned me to court a few months later, the same stranger promised that he would appear there as well. I had no way of knowing if he would follow through. He was an unknown to me, after all. How did I know if his word was good? What was I going to do if he left me hanging?

But he showed up. He told the judge what had happened and helped to exonerate me from accusations of reckless driving.

One of the coolest things about God is how He does everything He says He'll do. When He told Mary that she was going to give birth to His Son, despite the fact that she was still pure, sure enough! Nine months later...a Savior. And when He told Noah to start building that ark so that he and his family were ready when the rains came, He wasn't fooling around. Can you imagine Noah's relief when, after months of ridicule from those around him, the sky actually opened up and started to pour relentlessly for the very first time?

The Word is brimming with blotted stains of sin, promises about the future, and repentant new beginnings, each of them foretold by the very mouth of a loving God. Like Mary and Noah and so many others, we know that a promise made by the mouth of God is certain to be a promise kept. So when our Father tells us that He has plans for us, to bring us a future and a hope...or when He declares the cleansing of our sins because of what Jesus has done for us and He promises a place for us in heaven...thankfully, it's a done deal. ✳ *SDB*

Today's Prayer

Lord Jesus, thank You so much for being a God of Your Word!
Help me today to follow Your lead and become
the kind of person whose promise made is a promise kept.
In Your precious name I pray, amen.

I'm Not Scared
of the Dark...Much!

He setteth an end to darkness,
and searcheth out all perfection.

JOB 28:3 KJV

My neighborhood went completely dark this morning. No phone, no lights, no coffeepot, no computer. The power company's recorded message (retrieved thanks to a fully-charged cell phone) promised to return service by suppertime. If not for the delicate newborn grandchild I was babysitting, lack of creature comforts wouldn't be a problem.

As dads up and down the street tried to heft their garage doors without power openers, the elderly woman on the corner came to mind. Confined to a wheelchair, her television and radio are like friends who came to visit and never went home. Some of her medications require refrigeration, and she relies on electricity to keep her oxygen machine humming, too. A year or so ago, her kids gave her a generator for Christmas...but who would make sure there was enough gas in the tank to power it until the lights came back on? Who would run the cord to connect it to her life-saving machine? And how would I find out, when, without electricity, her phone wasn't working?

After bundling the baby, I headed up the street to check things out, praying, as the stroller squeaked over bumps and cracks in the sidewalk, that I'd get there in time to assure and calm her before taking care of things.

As I climbed the brick steps leading to her front door, her porch light flashed on and I heard the drone of the TV weatherman, who was promising a bright and sunny day. My elderly neighbor opened the door for us and, dragging a dozen feet of flexible clear tubing behind her, sang, "Come in! Sit down! And introduce me to that perfect little grandbaby of yours!"

While she crooned to the baby, I fixed us both a cup of tea and said a quiet prayer to the Father, who had known even before I left the house that the dear woman wouldn't need my help in hooking up her generator. What she needed that morning, as it turned out, was the living, breathing proof that the neighbors who so often said, "If you need anything, just call!" were thinking of her.

There were tears in her eyes when I returned to her living room with that tray of tea and cookies. "Just looking into a baby's innocent face is sure to start the waterworks," she said into a lace-trimmed hanky.

But I knew better. Oh, the baby might have inspired a little of the dampness, but the tears sparkling in her hazel eyes had been put there by joy and gratitude, and it humbled me to the soles of my sneakers.

I promised myself, even before handing her a teacup, that I'd make a point to visit her more often. Not just when the lights went out, but for no reason other than to help her pass an hour or two in that big, lonely house of hers.

And they say God works in mysterious ways! ✳ *LL*

Today's Prayer

Dear Lord, my God, I'm so grateful for Your unending patience! You knew even before I did how I'd react to the darkness...and that instead of trusting You to take care of Your children—even those who are well into their eighties—I'd rush out and try to take care of things myself. Thank You for giving me concrete examples and reminders that You are ever-watchful...and that something as simple as gazing upon the face of a newborn is so perfect that it can brighten an old woman's day. Amen.

It's a Jungle Out There

Have no fear of sudden disaster
or of the ruin that overtakes the wicked,
for the LORD will be your confidence
and will keep your foot from being snared.

PROVERBS 3:25–26 NIV

When I turned on the news a few minutes ago, I saw a five-car pileup between my house and where I used to work. I'm not surprised, because traffic in my area has gotten out of hand. I'm happy to be home working in my now-married daughter's old bedroom-turned-office.

Commuting to work has become a problem. What used to be a pleasant half-hour drive listening to a favorite CD or radio station has turned into a road-rage-filled free-for-all to the office, where other people sit at their desks snarling after a similar experience. This is not a good way to start *or* end the day.

It's been more than a year since I worked full-time and had to drive in rush-hour traffic, but I haven't forgotten what it's like. And if I ever did forget, all I'd have to do is listen to my husband or daughter Lauren and they'd remind me; they still have to deal with it.

I had some harrowing experiences while commuting. I saw road rage on a daily basis. People cut each other off, tailgated, and made obscene gestures. At times, I wondered if these people were always this way or if they acted out only when they were behind the wheel. Once I was rear-ended while stopped at a traffic light. Fortunately, there was minimal damage to both cars. I have to admit to a little fear after that. I held my breath at each light, watching in the rearview mirror and praying that the car behind me would stop.

There are so many things that can get us into trouble—things much worse than fender benders—and we constantly need to remember who we are as Christians. Focusing on the big picture of our desire for eternal life with our Father in heaven should be enough. When people offer that crude, all-too-familiar hand sign as they blow past us on the road, we need to take a few seconds and pray for them rather than get as upset as they are. If we're keeping Christ at the center of our lives, all the traffic in the world shouldn't rattle us. It's just a small, insignificant blip on the screen. ✻ DM

Today's Prayer

Lord, lead me through life without fear, and give me the ability
to focus on and trust You. As long as my eyes are on You,
I have the protection I need. Amen.

Even Muddy Water?

But Jesus said to him, "Do not forbid him,
for he who is not against us is on our side."

LUKE 9:50 NKJV

I happened to overhear a singer on TV belting out something about being baptized in muddy water. Curious, I paused at making dinner. After all, it's not often you hear about getting washed clean in amazing grace on primetime.

"This is way too electric for me," my husband complained from his recliner. He held up the remote, intending to change the channel.

"Hold on. I want to hear."

"It's bad music."

"Listen to the words," I argued. "It's a redemption song."

He grudgingly acquiesced.

The singer, who I later learned was Trace Adkins, crooned in his deep, rusty voice about how he hadn't been living like he "oughta" and how he wanted to drown that part of him in "muddy wata" (i.e., get baptized in the river behind his hometown's country church).

When Mr. Adkins and his band finished playing the tune (which, I thought, had quite the moving melody), I felt rather inspired. A second later, four people who are exceptionally near-and-dear to me came to mind. I knew they listened to country music on a regular basis. I'd been praying for them for years. They had walked away from God and lost their faith.

But there's always a way back. It just takes a rotation of the thought process. But how does that start? How does a person begin changing his or her thinking? I know how it happened for me—and keeps happening—but what about my loved ones?

Hearing the song, I wondered what would happen if these four special people heard this tune and realized they needed a little muddy water, too? Could God really use a country-western hit that was "way too electric" for my husband to reach them?

Immediately I was reminded that nothing is impossible for God (Luke 1:37). He can use people, places, songs, and inanimate objects as a sort of loving tap on the shoulder to say, "Follow Me.... My yoke is easy and My burden is light.... I am the way, the truth, and the life...." (Luke 5:27, Matthew 11:30, John 14:6 NKJV).

I felt encouraged. It's true: God can use whatever He pleases.... Yep, even muddy water! ✳ AKB

Today's Prayer

Dearest heavenly Father, You are the Almighty God, Creator of all.
You know our hearts. Please use whatever it takes to bring us closer to You
so we can truly experience Your unconditional love, amazing grace,
and divine forgiveness. In Christ's name, amen.

Un-Ring That Bell

See then that you walk circumspectly,
not as fools but as wise....
EPHESIANS 5:15 NKJV

A dear friend of mine recently received the final papers dissolving her twelve-year marriage.

I ordered Chinese takeout and took it over to her house that night so she wouldn't be alone. I didn't know what to say to comfort her, but her weepy disposition clearly declared that she needed comforting.

"The worst part," she told me later that same evening, "is that I can tell you the exact moment when my marriage ended. And it was my fault."

Dara and her husband, Eric, argued often. But on this one occasion, they let the momentum of their disagreement build instead of taking off to separate corners. Both of them said things they shouldn't have, and both of them behaved in ways unbecoming of a couple striving toward spending their lives together.

"We didn't speak to one another for three days after that," she said. "In my frustration, I rang the bell."

"The bell?" I asked.

"The one you can't un-ring. I said I wanted a divorce."

It was a snowball rolling down a hill. Dara and Eric both shifted into OVERDRIVE and began behaving according to emotion. Eric eventually moved out, and Dara was the first to visit an attorney. Now, a year later, here she sat in a small rental apartment, wondering why she'd let it all go so horribly wrong.

Emotions can be so dangerous, especially when we don't realize that we have a choice. We can follow them and let them guide the direction of our lives, or we can choose to set our feelings aside long enough to rule them rather than allowing them to rule us.

The better part of wisdom comes in understanding that our future will be decided by the choices we make. Stepping back, cooling off, and making an informed, intelligent decision, rather than ringing a bell that can never be un-rung, will make for a much more peaceful tomorrow.

✳ SDB

Today's Prayer

Father, thank You for Your loving grace. In that grace, help me today to be wise and to take authority over my emotions rather than allow them to take authority over me. In Jesus' holy name I pray, amen.

Rocky Mountain College

Therefore shall ye lay up these my words in your heart and in your soul....
Ye shall teach them Your children, speaking of them when thou
sittest in thine house, and when thou walkest by the way,
when thou liest down, and when thou risest up.

DEUTERONOMY 11:18–19 KJV

Cowboys and mountain men of yore weren't known for spouting philosophy or quoting Shakespeare, but a whole whoppin' bunch of 'em coulda been!

It took a long time, see, for the snow to melt and the rivers to thaw, confining them to cabins with little more to do than read. Scouring now-abandoned camps, lucky (if not nosy) tourists have stumbled upon yellowing editions of Keats, Scott, Wordsworth, James Fenimore Cooper, Jonathan Smith, and more.

Picture, if you will, a whiskered gent sipping thick black coffee by the light of an oil lantern. Shoulders cloaked by a bearskin blanket, he warms his fur-shod feet near the fire and teaches an illiterate bunkmate to read, using the Good Book as his how-to manual. They called this time, sealed away from civilization as they were, days at Rocky Mountain College.

Like those miners and buckskinners, I've survived many a bitter winter in much the same way, though admittedly my boots are faux fur and the blanket around my shoulders is microsuede. And though I'm usually free to hop into my trusty car and blaze the trails laid out by snowplows and salt trucks, the power lines have fallen enough times that I can readily identify with having to read by the light of a kerosene lamp, with the woodstove as my heat source.

Books are like friends, all with different looks and scents. But whether tall or fat, thin or squat, the pages bound between their covers promise to entertain, educate, enlighten, and inform. And the book that starts and ends every day—whether the snow barely covers the soles of my shoes or threatens to spill into my knee-high boots—is the Bible.

Thanks to a hearty concordance, I'm never far from solutions to my problems. Though the bowl of popcorn on my lap overflows, even the buttery-est kernels can't satisfy me in quite the same way as the stories in the gilt-edged pages of the Book.

The weather outside is snowing, but as winter gentles to spring, I hope I'll remember the verse from Jeremiah 15:16 that goes, "When your words came, I ate them; they were my joy and my heart's delight, for I bear your name, O Lord God Almighty" (NIV), and take comfort from unrelenting rains and summer's drought and the hurricanes of autumn...

...so I'll show the world just what a Rocky Mountain College graduate is capable of! ✳ $\mathcal{LL}$

Today's Prayer

I read today that You cured lepers, Lord—nine of them—
and each one forgot to thank You! It's easy to see
their faults and failings, but I pray that I'll never become
so embroiled in my own wants and needs that I forget
it's You who provides my every need. Bless me, gentle Jesus,
with a grateful heart and a faithful spirit. Amen.

LOL and ROTFL

Then our mouth was filled with laughter, and our tongue with singing.
Then they said among the nations, "The LORD has done great things for them."
PSALM 126:2 NKJV

I'd feel lost without e-mail and IM. I love being able to stay in communication with friends and family all over the world. And how fun to be able to show when I'm laughing with a ☺ or a *LOL*. What did we ever do before the Internet?

More than twenty years ago, my family moved from Florida to Tennessee in the middle of January. The day before the movers arrived with all our worldly possessions, there was a snowstorm like one I'd never seen—and I've never liked cold weather. Within the first year of moving there, all of us got sick, my mother became an invalid, we realized our house was a money pit, and my husband lost his job due to a downturn in the economy. I felt like it couldn't get any worse. Fortunately, I was right.

Our lives are like roller-coasters of joy, sorrow, and everything in between, and it's easy to get caught up in worry and frustration. Sometimes it seems like bad things come in multiples, making each day more miserable than the last. Our blinders often prevent us from seeing the fun and humor surrounding us.

As Christians, we look forward to eternal joy and freedom from suffering, God's promise. As we go through our days, we need to remember to LOL and ROTFL every chance we get. ✽ *DM*

Today's Prayer

Lord, I'm grateful for the joy and happiness in my life.
Allow me to focus on Your goodness, even when times get rough. Amen.

Bing! The Light Bulb Goes On

"I now send you, to open their eyes, in order to turn them
from darkness to light, and from the power of Satan to God,
that they may receive forgiveness of sins and an inheritance
among those who are sanctified by faith in Me."

ACTS 26:17–18 NKJV

One sunny winter morning as we drove to church, my husband, Daniel, reminisced about how we had taught third-grade Sunday school. We taught the same grade together for almost five years. I used to dislike all the preparation that went into it and the follow-up, but Daniel enjoyed each minute of it. He's got a gift with children.

One year a little girl began to cry when she learned that Daniel was her teacher. At first glance my husband looks like a big, stern guy, but he's really a gentle giant with a huge heart and lots of patience. A month later, the same little girl came to trust and admire "Mr. Boeshaar" and even made him homemade Christmas ornaments that we hang on our tree to this day. Now that little girl is a young woman attending a Christian college!

"You sure are an old man," I teased Daniel. Then I saw the grin form under his mustache.

As we passed farm fields blanketed in snow, Daniel remarked how much he enjoyed seeing "the light go on" when children in our class understood the biblical concept he was presenting. "Their eyes lit up," he said. "It was so rewarding for me when I reached them like that."

"You impacted a lot of lives."

"Well, so did you."

I think about some of the kids in my classes, too. Even now when I see "my kids," all grown up in the hallways at church, I can tell that they remember I was once their fun-loving Sunday school teacher.

As much as I thought it was a pain to get ready for class, teaching Sunday school was a rewarding experience for me, too. I remember when I taught a lesson on baptism. One little girl in my class caught the meaning and wanted to be baptized. Her parents were so happy, and one Sunday night Naomi was baptized while I watched from a pew inside the sanctuary. I'll never forget how awed I felt that God would use me to reach a little girl with His truth. I guess I took the power of teaching for granted—when in actuality it's a privilege! ✳ AKB

Today's Prayer

Heavenly Father, thank You for using us as instruments of Your love.
May You continue to use us to bring people in, from the darkness to the Light,
that they may understand all the love, joy, and peace You afford.
In Christ's name, amen!

An Elephant Never Forgets!

Brethren, I do not count myself to have apprehended;
but one thing I do, forgetting those things which are behind
and reaching forward to those things which are ahead,
I press toward the goal for the prize of the
upward call of God in Christ Jesus.

PHILIPPIANS 3:13–14 NKJV

Michael was just about the cutest boy I'd ever seen. He had dark, floppy, Hugh Grant kind of hair that still does me in to this day... and crystal blue eyes that peered right through the window to my soul. The moment I laid eyes on him, I fell in love.

Fifteen-year-old kind of love, anyway.

And the worst part was...he was the boyfriend of one of my closest friends. I saw them together at dances and parties and barbecues. It was enough to shatter my teenage heart into a million tiny pieces.

One night at a swim party, Michael brought me a glass of soda. Just as he handed it to me, he leaned in and kissed me. My heart soared, my knees grew weak, and my equilibrium fell right over. And then I looked up to find my friend, his girlfriend, standing in the doorway and watching us in horror.

She never spoke to me again after that incident. When I ran into her again ten years later, after she was married with two children, it turned out that she still wasn't speaking to me.

"It's kind of water under the bridge, isn't it?" I asked, trying to get her to communicate with me. "Neither one of us ended up with Michael, and we were just teenagers anyway."

"An elephant never forgets," she finally said.

"But...you're not...an elephant," I replied.

It didn't matter that her nose was small and upturned and not shaped like a trunk. She turned on her heel, grabbed her daughter's hand, and marched out of the shop with that nose right up in the air—and without another word to me.

It just broke my heart that something done out of teenaged ignorance had pierced my old friend so deeply that she'd been carrying it with her all those years. I thought about calling her, urging her to listen to reason, but something within me warned against it. Going forward is almost always the better choice, even if someone else seems stuck in the past. ✳ *SDB*

Today's Prayer

Lord Jesus, thank You for the forgiving and sanctifying sacrifice
You gave so that I would not be buried by my own past mistakes.
Help me to render Your kind of grace to those around me
who may need the forgiveness that my heart doesn't want to give.
In Your precious name I pray, amen.

Alternatives, Options, and Choices

Make me to go in the path of thy commandments;
for therein do I delight.
PSALM 119:35 KJV

*B*aseball great Yogi Berra earned more fame for his witty quotes than his expertise on the field, and the Berra-cism closest to my heart goes like this: "When you come to a fork in the road, take it."

I'm a great believer in motivational stuff, which explains why mottos like Yogi's surround my computer monitor. The rainbow of Post-it Notes that frame the screen make it possible—unconsciously, at least—for me to keep the good advice in mind as I work. I'll let you decide if their similarities are more funny than amazing, or if it's the other way around:

- "The turtle only makes progress when he chooses to stick his neck out" (James Bryant).
- "Excellence is not an accident; it's a choice" (Unknown).
- "Heaven on earth is a choice we make, not a place we find" (Wayne Dyer).
- "We are happy if we choose to be" (Alexander Solzhenitsyn).
- "The strongest principle of growth lies in human choice" (George Eliot).
- "Life is like a box of chocolates; you never know what you're gonna get" (Forrest Gump).
- "No one can tell us how much to give; the only safe rule is, give more than [you] can spare" (C. S. Lewis).

- "Tact is the art of choosing to make guests feel comfortable in your home when you really wish they were elsewhere" (George E. Bergman).
- "Before you choose to criticize someone, walk a mile in their shoes. That way, when you're finished, you're a mile away... and you have their shoes" (Frieda Norris).

Every day, a thousand times over, I'm forced to make choices: White bread or rye? Light or heavy starch? Take that call, or let the answering machine get it? Paper or plastic? Like ripples in a pond, everything I say and do (or decide not to say or do) has far-reaching effects not only on me but on everyone I come into contact with. No wonder Mom spent so much time trying to teach me that with each choice comes its own set of personal responsibilities!

So whether I choose to donate an old sofa to a home for battered women or bite my tongue when someone offends me, there are consequences...some that fill me with dread and others that leave me overjoyed.

How blessed I am to have a Lord who will help me make Christian choices, whether I call upon Him once or a thousand times! ✳ *LL*

Today's Prayer

O God Most High, I praise You for knowing this servant so well!
Every thought in my head, every dream in my heart is heard by You long
before my mind forms the words. Bless me, O Savior, with the will to make
choices that are pleasing to You, every day and in every way. Amen.

Love Me,
Love My Baggage

"And you shall not only show me the kindness of the LORD while I still live,
that I may not die; but you shall not cut off your kindness from my house forever,
no, not when the LORD has cut off every one of the enemies of David
from the face of the earth."

1 SAMUEL 20:14–15 NKJV

I grew up in a non-Christian home. Notice I didn't say "anti-Christian." My parents just didn't see the need for church, other than the occasional Easter and Christmas services. My mother claimed to believe in God, but she never spoke about her relationship with the Lord. My father didn't like to talk about faith issues at all. But at an early age, I knew that something was missing.

My father was a career air force man, which instantly made me a "military brat"—a term I now realize isn't the worst thing. Brats are spunky survivors, even if they are...well, brats. We moved often, which was both good and bad. I saw and did things most children never have the opportunity to experience. I also had to guard my heart when we picked up and moved away from friends I'd never see again. That was rough. Each time we relocated, my parents settled in with new jobs, but it was never that easy for me. I had to go through the entire process of learning about others and trying to fit in. However, I always knew in the back of my mind that I'd have to move again, so I never let anyone get too close; it would simply be too painful when I had to go somewhere else.

There were other issues that probably had a lot to do with the military. My father had temporary duty assignments that took him away from my mother and me for extended periods of time. I didn't see him for a couple of years when I was a toddler, so when he came back home, I was leery. Not long after I graduated from college, my parents divorced, which rattled my young adult life to the core.

Throughout my childhood, I met people who believed in the Lord—some of them military brats who attended services at the nondenominational base chapel. Others were locals who'd gone to the same church all their lives. I was fortunate enough to be invited, and it was there that I saw what was most important in this world. I learned that through faith in Christ, we have a home with God.

When my husband and I first met, there was an instant attraction, but we were both cautious. During one of our early conversations, he told me that he didn't want to pursue a relationship with me unless I was a believer. Fortunately, Christ had already become a vital part of my life, even without my parents' assistance. We had issues to overcome—our emotional baggage from the past—but our common faith in Christ led us to where we are today.

Everyone has baggage. However, God has promised us salvation through Christ, so that baggage is checked at the door when we enter His kingdom. ✳ DM

Today's Prayer

Thank You, Lord, for accepting us as we are—baggage and all. I pray that
I will serve You by loving and helping others who feel unworthy of
Your many blessings. In Your holy name, Jesus, amen.

From Rock 'n' Roll to the Solid Rock

He has put a new song in my mouth.
PSALM 40:3 NKJV

About nineteen years ago, I was a rock 'n' roll junkie. I knew the names of performers and singer-songwriters, the history of their careers and their rock bands. I'd wake up to my music, and if I heard my song, that meant I'd have a good day. The lyrics influenced my decisions, which, in turn, affected my abilities as a mother and a wife. I'd listen to my music at work, to and from work, and blare it from my speakers at home. This music was my driving force, the essence of my very being.

But then God saved me. I didn't think much of my music at first. I added God to it. I suppose I figured God was cool and changed with the times. Then I learned God is "the same yesterday, today, and forever" (Hebrews 13:8 NKJV). Soon after that, the Lord showed me that the lyrics of the tunes I so enjoyed contradicted His Word. The music itself was an idol in my life, and it became apparent to me that I needed to give it up.

I made the choice to obey the Holy Spirit.

One night our church had an Acts 19:19 party, at which we burned our "curious art," as the King James Version refers to it. We piled up all our books and record albums, CDs, videos—anything belonging to us that we felt had hindered our walk with Christ. The pile was huge, and if someone had estimated its worth, I'm sure it would have been thousands of dollars. Sure, we could have sold the items and given the cash to the church; however, burning the items seemed so symbolic for many of us. These possessions had us under a kind of spell that kept us separated from the love of Christ.

For me, the Lord put a new song in my mouth.

My hope is built on nothing less
Than Jesus' blood and righteousness.
I dare not trust the sweetest frame
But wholly lean on Jesus' name.

On Christ the solid Rock, I stand—
All other ground is sinking sand.

Edward Mote, 1797–1874

✻ *AKB*

Today's Prayer

Precious Lord God, we thank You for removing obstacles
from our lives that steal the time, love, and joy we should
be giving to You. Sometimes it doesn't seem fair
when You remove these prized possessions or favored habits
from us, but after we replace them with You,
the blessings that rain down from heaven
are too numerous to count. Give us the wisdom and courage, Lord,
to give You the first and highest priority in our busy lives.

Monsters in the Shadows

Have I not commanded you?
Be strong and of good courage;
do not be afraid, nor be dismayed,
for the LORD your God is with you wherever you go.

JOSHUA 1:9 NKJV

had a part-time job for a while at the children's photography studio of a department store. It was a great job. I loved working with the kids, and I quickly developed a reputation as the only photographer on staff who could get the really young babies to smile. I'd set them in place, talk to them while I prepped the camera, and then make some funny noises to snag their wide-eyed attention.

The studio faced out into the mall, and I'd often draw a crowd of onlookers with those ridiculous noises when working a later shift. Sometimes I would even notice a couple of the same faces back to watch the action.

One night, I decided to go out for coffee with a friend after work, and I returned home fairly late. My upstairs neighbor trotted down the stairs to meet me at my door.

"Hey, listen," he said, "I just wanted to let you know that there was a very strange guy outside your back door earlier."

Dennis had come across the stranger and asked him what he was doing behind the condo building where I lived. He said he was looking for the woman who worked at the photography studio—and he didn't use my name.

"I told him you weren't home," Dennis explained, "and that he would have to come back another time. He was kind of creepy, wearing this battered army jacket with patches on the arm."

I immediately thought of one of those returning faces in the crowd outside of the studio. I'd seen him there at least three times that week, and *creepy* was a perfect word to describe him.

A week later, I was watching the local news when they aired footage of a serial rapist who had just been captured. The dark-haired man being led into a police cruiser was wearing a torn T-shirt beneath a very familiar army jacket.

"What if I hadn't decided to go out for coffee?" I asked Dennis afterward. "I would have been home that night."

"Somebody was looking out for you, that's for sure," he replied. I just smiled, knowing full well who that Somebody was. ✳ *SDB*

Today's Prayer

Thank You, Lord, for Your protection, even when I don't know
I'm in need of it. Help me today to remember that I am cupped
in the palm of Your hand and that You can see around every dark corner
and into the shadows where danger hides. I am protected by Your grace.
In Your holy name I pray, amen.

And the Award Goes to...

Nor did we seek glory from men,
either from you or from others,
when we might have made demands....

1 THESSALONIANS 2:6 NKJV

I can't think of a single person who isn't at least *a little bit* competitive. Andy Warhol wasn't just whistlin' "Dixie" when he declared that no matter who we are or what we do, we crave our fifteen minutes of fame.

It isn't sinful, after all, to want some recognition when we accomplish something. In fact, it's part of human nature to work *toward* earning awards, accolades, and praise.

Tiger Woods wants another green jacket. Andy Murray yearns for a tennis Grand Slam. The Steelers will "Terrible Towel" teams that try to keep them out of the Super Bowl, while the Phillies dream of repeating their World Series win. Brad Pitt can almost feel that Oscar in his hands, and Robert Plant can already hear his name being called at the Grammys.

And on less world-renowned stages, everyday mortals picture themselves at the podium, thanking everyone from their maiden aunt Olive to the mailman for whichever laurels have been bestowed. Authors hope that their novels will appear on bookstore shelves, and parents long to accept PTA presidential nominations. Members of the Ladies' Auxiliary secretly want credit for every dollar raised to buy the church a new organ.

I repeat: It isn't a sin to desire a bit of honor for a job well done. *Bu–u–ut...*

Personally, I get into trouble when I put "respect my deed" ahead of the deed itself...and forget who is responsible for my ability to compete in the first place! Working all day, every day, at a job that demands solitude makes it doubly pleasurable when others sing my praises, and it doesn't much matter whether they come in the form of rave reviews or certificates or letters from my readers!

For me, zeroing in too tightly on what comes *after* the work is done distracts me. And that's why I quickly file away the physical evidence of that stuff and grab my Bible.

It's amazing how quickly I feel invigorated and inspired once I've reminded myself that none of it—the work or the awards—belongs to me, but to Him who blessed me with the talent to do it and the drive to achieve it. ✳ *LL*

Today's Prayer

My Lord, never let me forget that while the world continues to sort its
residents into groups of "the great" and "those who bow to greatness,"
You open Your arms to every one of Your children, every second they are alive!
Thank You, Jesus, for keeping me ever-humble, so that my pride
will never offend You. Amen.

Not All News Is Spam

And the LORD passed before him and proclaimed, "The LORD, the LORD God,
merciful and gracious, longsuffering, and abounding in goodness and truth,
keeping mercy for thousands, forgiving iniquity and transgression and sin, by no
means clearing the guilty, visiting the iniquity of the fathers upon the children
and the children's children to the third and the fourth generation."

EXODUS 34:6–7 NKJV

The first thing I do every morning is turn on the computer and let it boot up while I get my first cup of coffee ready. Then I sit down and delete all my spam e-mail before I read any of the relevant messages and news—something sent just to me.

I find most spam to be very annoying, and I grumble about its intrusion. Why would ABC Bank want me to "click here" to validate personal information on an account I never had? Why would I want to buy a college degree online after I spent long hours studying and boatloads of my parents' money for a real one? How can I win a lottery I didn't even enter?

We get spam in various forms; however, one place you won't find spam is the Bible.

As I read today's scripture verse, I think about the impact of God's proclamation. All other news pales compared to this holy broadcast. Every single word of it is important; there is absolutely nothing that should be deleted. In other words, there's not a bit of spam in the Bible.
✳ DM

Today's Prayer

Heavenly Father, Your news is the best news of all. Keep me focused on Your Word and help me filter everything that doesn't bring me closer to You. Amen.

I Have the Pow–wer!

*"Behold, I give you the authority to trample on serpents and scorpions, and over all
the power of the enemy, and nothing shall by any means hurt you.
Nevertheless do not rejoice in this, that the spirits are subject to you,
but rather rejoice because your names are written in heaven."*

LUKE 10:19–20 NKJV

When my sons were little, they enjoyed watching "Masters of the Universe." These cartoons starred He-Man, who would hold up his sword to the sky and proclaim, "I have the pow–wer...." Lightning flashed, thunder rumbled, and suddenly He-Man had the ability to take on the bad guys and win.

As Christians we really do have the "pow–wer." Jesus Christ has given it to us. No situation is insurmountable for believers in Him—not even evil spirits can stand against us. But the true battlefield is in the mind and the devil's desire is to disable each one of us, rendering us weak, fearful, and useless.

One of Satan's favorite tricks is to play back those proverbial "tapes" in our head. You know, the ones that go, "You'll never amount to anything" or "You're not pretty enough." Before long we're suffocating beneath a dark cloak of discouragement.

But we can lift our sword of the Spirit, which is the Word of God (see Ephesians 6:13–17), and suddenly we can be triumphant! ✳ AKB

Today's Prayer

Dearest Lord God, thank You for giving us the power to live victorious lives.
Thank You for Your love and protection. We're never alone and never unarmed.

The *C* Word

*For I know the thoughts that I think toward you,
says the LORD, thoughts of peace and not of evil,
to give you a future and a hope.*

JEREMIAH 29:11 NKJV

There are a few words in the English language that just seem to take folks by surprise. People don't want to say the words, and they don't want to hear them. At the top of that vocabulary list is the most terrible one of all: *Cancer*.

My mom used to whisper the word, as if saying it quietly would take away a bit of its punch.

"His wife passed away last year," she would say. And then, cupping her hands around her mouth, she would whisper, "Breast cancer."

There was one Sunday afternoon, years after my mom had died, that I found myself wishing she had taught this fine art of whispering to my doctor.

"I'm so sorry," she told me. "It's Stage 3 ovarian cancer."

There was more, I think. Something about the best course of treatment and surgery to be scheduled right away, but I didn't hear most of it. Cradling the phone under my chin, I wondered, *If she'd whispered it, would it have been Stage 2 instead?*

Over that one weekend, my life went from meetings, sales figures, and workshops to one small, dark tunnel in the shape of a *C*. My job and writing career were a thing of the past, replaced in an instant by the three surgeries that followed the diagnosis and then five weeks of daily radiation treatments, medications that made me sick, and headaches that could make a grown woman cry "Uncle."

I remember a particular day about four weeks into my treatments.... I'd climbed up onto the table and nurses buzzed around me, lining up the radiation machine with the tattoos they'd placed on my pelvis a month earlier—and suddenly I was wiping tears from my face. I hadn't even realized I was crying! But as I wiped my cheek and sniffed back the next wave, it occurred to me that I was screaming. Not out loud, but from the inside. *Scrrreeeeeeeaming!*

All those weeks of surgeries and treatment, and the reality of the situation had never really set in until that very moment. And just about the time I was an instant away from flying off that table and out the front door of the center, my heart fluttered and a scripture came softly to mind:

> *"I know the thoughts that I think toward you, says the LORD,*
> *thoughts of peace and not of evil, to give you a future and a hope."*

In that strange and surreal moment, in the dark room of my cancer treatment center, I realized that the medical professionals flitting around me had very little to do with my diagnosis. It was up to my God whether I would live or die, and for the first time in a very, very long time, I knew with clear certainty that I was going to live. ✳ *SDB*

Today's Prayer

Thank You, Father, for Your assurance and love. I praise You for bringing me through the darkest days of my life and for lighting the way to the happiest ones. But mostly I want You to know that I am humbled and grateful that Your hand is upon me, promising me a future and a hope. In Jesus' name, amen.

When Life Gets Squirrelly...

For every beast of the forest is mine, and the cattle upon a thousand hills.
PSALM 50:10 KJV

Others might scold the squirrel who raids my bird feeders and eats more seeds than a flock of chickadees, but I enjoy his antics!

First he's a four-footed circus performer, scampering across power lines to the telephone pole to the tree near my feeder.

Next he's the Man on the Flying Trapeze, sailing through the air, aiming for the feeder...and his next free meal of black sunflower seeds.

Then he's an acrobat, hanging upside down to reach even more of the delectable treats, which are stored in a feeder that was advertised as a brand-new design and guaranteed to be "completely squirrel-proof."

Now he's the peeping Tom who stands on my windowsill, with his paws to the glass...his way of saying, "Hey, the feeder is empty."

Like the postman, he arrives in good weather and in bad, braving rain and snow and summer's blistering heat—and I can't help but admire his perseverance. As Christians, we could all do with a little of that attitude, because unlike the nutty squirrel, our God and Father answers prayers even if we don't perform silly tricks to entertain Him.

But He might just get a chuckle out of seeing me staring into His window while I wait for Him to meet my needs.... ✳ *LL*

Today's Prayer

Father, bless me with a heart that recognizes and appreciates every creature
You have made, and remind me to see the beauty in each one. Amen.

Chicken Little

Therefore I say to you, do not worry about your life,
what you will eat or what you will drink;
nor about your body, what you will put on.
Is not life more than food and the body more than clothing?

MATTHEW 6:25 NKJV

he sky is falling."

"If anything can go wrong, it will."

"All good things must come to an end."

How has so much negativity crept into our lives? You'd think that with all the commercials about "Having it your way" and "You deserve the very best," we'd all be glowing with radiant joy.

My mother was a child of the Great Depression, so she constantly talked about having enough food to eat. Some of that rubbed off on me, and I still worry—even though I have a full refrigerator, enough clothes in my closet to not wear the same thing twice in a month, and possessions that can keep me occupied 24/7.

While grocery shopping, my mother was a woman on a mission—determined to provide for her family with the resolve that each meal might be our last if we didn't stock up and prepare for some unknown disaster.

"Why are you buying so much soup?" I once asked my mom, as she transferred two of each kind of Campbell's Soup from the store shelf to the basket.

"You never know when you'll run out," she replied as she turned the basket toward the household items to stock up on toilet paper.

With the innocence of a child, I tilted my head and studied the soup before turning back to her. "Can't we just buy some more?"

She tossed a multi-roll pack of toilet paper into the cart, quirked one corner of her mouth, frowned, shook her head, and pushed the basket toward the Spam, making me feel like my question didn't deserve an answer. I now understand that she didn't have an answer, and one thing she wasn't willing to say was that she didn't know something about the future—which brings me to my point: Does anyone know what the future brings?

I certainly don't. No matter how much I plan, anything can happen. The future is out of my control, which sometimes irks me because I seem to have turned into my mother. And yes, sometimes I feel like the sky is falling.

Now my firstborn has a child, and I see that the world is still intact. My daughter is doing some of the same things I did as a young mother— trying her best to create a perfect world to keep the sky from falling.

We need to stop worrying about the future and trust God with everything. ✳ DM

Today's Prayer

You've provided my family with so many blessings, Lord. I know I don't have a reason to worry—and I thank You. Each day brings new challenges, but You always provide for us. Please give me the ability to be calm and accept all of Your blessings with the right spirit. Amen.

Taking It to the Top

"If my people who are called by My name
will humble themselves, and pray
and seek My face, and turn from their wicked ways,
then I will hear from heaven, and will forgive their sin and heal their land."

2 CHRONICLES 7:14 NKJV

Last week I kissed my twenty-seven-year-old son good-bye. I won't see him for a whole year. He and his wife both serve in the Army National Guard. They boarded a plane for Texas. From there they'll ship off to Iraq.

My mother's heart is breaking. This is Brian's second tour overseas.

War. I hate it. In fact, I wouldn't allow my sons to play with guns and GI Joe action figures when they were little boys. The violence of war runs against the grain of my very nature. But here's my "baby," leaving the country with the Army National Guard.

My mother's heart breaks just a little more, although I'm the first to declare that our troops are heroes and I do respect what they're doing overseas. I'm a supporter of the United States military. It might seem oxymoronic; however, somehow I've been able to separate and rationalize. What's more, I call myself a patriot even though I still buy into that old 1960s saying that "war is not healthy for children and other living things." Perhaps you could say I'm for it while being against it.

Oh, brother! Now I sound like a politician!

Okay, well, I'll admit there are things in the political arena that I feel strongly about, but I'm not a political activist, and yet God calls me to speak out against that which I feel is unjust. However, He doesn't lead me, personally, to protest and carry picket signs, although He might lead others to do so. No, the Lord calls me to activism on my knees. God says if I humble myself and pray and seek His face, He will hear me from heaven and heal my land.

You know, much can be accomplished when we bow the knee. Abraham pleaded with the Lord to spare his nephew Lot's life before God destroyed Sodom and Gomorrah. God heard Abraham's prayer and sent His angels to rescue Lot (Genesis 19).

Jesus Himself tells of how God can be persuaded by persistent prayer. He said we should pray and not lose heart; God will bring about justice (Luke 18).

So what's troubling you today? Global issues? Our country's state of affairs? A family crisis? Whatever it is, the Lord is waiting for you—and for me—to get on our knees, seek His face, and pray. ✳ *AKB*

Today's Prayer

Dear Father God, our world seems like such a mess. But You are the Creator of all. You alone can turn people's hearts from greed to giving, from evil to good. Lord, we praise You for who You are, and we ask for Your amazing grace in this unsettling time. Shelter us from harm. Keep us safe in the storms of life. We will give You all the glory for it. In Jesus' precious name, amen.

Wait Is a Four-Letter Word

Be still, and know that I am God.
PSALM 46:10 NKJV

The neighborhood luminaria was a tradition. Every Christmas Eve before the big family dinner, my dad and I would go into the garage and fill paper bags with sand. Then we carried them out to the street and, measuring out five big teenage-sized steps between them, plopped down the bags along the edge of our property line. Then it was my job to carefully plant one candle into each bag. After dinner, right at dusk, we'd go outside, bundled up with coats and gloves and scarves, and light the candles with the neighbors so that the entire neighborhood was outlined with a magical Christmas Eve luminaria. It's my favorite Christmas memory.

For several years, it was just about all I could do to get through dinner. I wanted to light those candles so badly!

"You don't want to light them too early," my mom explained. "You want them to blend in with the rest of the neighborhood. That's why everyone lights them at the same time."

But I didn't care about blending or the neighborhood, and certainly not about waiting! I just wanted to see those beautiful lights flickering along the bottom of the hill next to our road.

One year, I was able to talk my dad into letting me light the candles before dinner. It was going to snow, I reasoned. It made sense to light the candles beforehand. When my father finally agreed, I was jubilant and ran out of the house without a coat, flicking the lighter before I ever reached the bottom of the drive.

But the truth is...it was a bit of a letdown. Ours was the only house flanked by the luminaria lights, and although it was lovely, I was really struck by the difference later that night when our neighbors joined in and the unbroken trail of lights circled the entire block and curved around the steep hill at the edge of our neighborhood. I admitted that night that I wished I'd waited. I think it must have been music to my mother's ears.

Waiting is such a difficult thing, especially when the prize is well within our sight. But I've learned over the years that there is actually a joy in learning to wait. There is delicious anticipation, never knowing what God might do at the last minute to surprise you.

"Be still, and know that I am God," His Word tells us. But today He might say to us, "Be still and put your feet up. Think about something else. Let your nail polish dry! Be still and wait to see how I'm going to dazzle you." ✳ SDB

Today's Prayer

Father, thank You for Your reminder that there is a time and season
for every good thing You have for me. Help me today to rest in Your peace,
enjoy the moment, and step into pace with Your timing.
In the holy name of Jesus I pray, amen.

A Cut Above

I am the true vine, and my Father is the husbandman.
Every branch in me that beareth not fruit he taketh away:
and every branch that beareth fruit,
he purgeth it, that it may bring forth more fruit.

JOHN 15:1-2 KJV

I'm the first to admit I know diddly about growing grapes—or any other kind of fruit, for that matter. But trial and error *has* taught me a thing or three about caring for roses. I have a dozen lovely rosebushes out back, each a different color, variety, and temperament. Some produce gorgeous flowers with little more than sunshine and rainfall, while others require supreme effort and patience to bloom.

The toughest part of my job as a "cultivator" is knowing *when* to go at the shrubs with sharp pruning shears and *which* branches to lop off. Some make it easy for me, by displaying spindly growth or disease. Others make me look closer while trying to remember just how many blooms each produced.

Snipping off the dead stuff is a no-brainer. They're ugly. They drain the plant of energy as it tries to revive what's "gone bad." And let's face it: If they can't pump out pretty petals, what good are they?

SNIP!

After a heavy rain, some branches can grow long and scraggly. They'll spit out a flower here and there, but those blooms won't be robust, and they won't last long, either.

SNIP!

Still other branches please the eye and nose with dozens of beautiful buds...but after a few weeks of that, they'll wear themselves out.

SNIP!

The Lord works miracles with His children in much the same way.

We rarely like seeing the flash of His pruning shears, and we like being the recipient of His snippers even less. But He knows what He's doing, and if we're honest with ourselves, we recognize how much we needed a little pruning.

I'm notorious for working long, grueling days to "grow" my writing career. But God's pruning has taught me that if I don't take time to care for my soul, myself, and my family, He's more than willing to lop at my so-called growth. Illness—nothing truly serious but enough to force me into quiet R & R—has been His method for reminding me of what's truly important. It's while I rest and recuperate that I slow down enough to count my blessings...and afterward, I'm more fruitful and productive than before!

Why is it, I wonder, that when times are tough, we eagerly fall to our knees—yet when things are going great, we think it's safe to stray... a little, anyway...from Him?

Maybe it's because we fear He'll see it's time to whip out those shears.... ✳ *L L*

Today's Prayer

Lord of all, I will succumb to Your practiced hand! Keep my whining
to a minimum as I endure the necessary pruning that will remove my
weaknesses and strengthen me. Watch over me so that I won't waste
the new growth You've encouraged, and bless me with a steadfastness
that ensures my life will branch out, producing the scents and blossoms
that will bring glory and honor to Your most holy Name. Amen.

My Big Fat American Dream

Better to be a nobody and yet have a servant than pretend to be somebody and have no food. A righteous man cares for the needs of his animal, but the kindest acts of the wicked are cruel. He who works his land will have abundant food, but he who chases fantasies lacks judgment.

PROVERBS 12:9–11 NIV

My big fat American dream has consumed me! I have a great house. We have more room than we need, the latest appliances, a yard filled with high-maintenance landscaping, and a welcoming porch that gives the impression that a hospitable family lives here—even though we don't even know some of our neighbors.

We have other great junk, too, like cars, TVs, and computers! Our kitchen is filled with all the coolest gadgets shown on the Food Network because "You never know when you might need a citrus zester."

So why am I so frazzled?

As I look at my life, I realize that the things my hard work has paid for have put me in bondage and won't let go unless I understand basic biblical principles. Taking a step back and looking at the big picture— what really matters most in our lives—I have to ask myself this obvious question: Will having the latest and greatest worldly things take us to our ultimate goal? If it's to die rich in the world's eyes, yes. But if it's to die in this world and reawaken with the Lord, absolutely not! And then I hear those words from Proverbs chapter 12.

Better to be a nobody and yet have a servant than pretend to be somebody and have no food.

Should I work hard? Of course.

He who works his land will have abundant food....

We work to live and enjoy His blessings, which are not of this world.
...but he who chases fantasies lacks judgment.

Say what? All those things I've worked so hard to attain are merely fantasies that show a lack of judgment? In a nutshell...yes.

So do I have to sell my house and all its contents and live a life of poverty in order to be godlier? Not unless I can't afford to maintain what I've already been blessed with. However, it is time for my husband and me to take stock of what we have and vow to appreciate everything the Lord has allowed us to bring into our lives. Then we need to focus on moving forward in a more faithful way and pray before we acquire anything new. Our children don't need most of what they have, but they do need to learn good stewardship—as do my husband and I.

Rather than spending time poring over catalogs and drooling over TV commercials, the time has come to begin each day with prayer, to be thankful, and to ask for guidance in every decision we make. We don't need to focus so much on what our money will buy but instead on working to the glory of the Lord.

I will be satisfied with my blessings and pray for Him to use me to do His will rather than my own. ✳ *DM*

Today's Prayer

Lord, thank You for the abundant blessings You've brought my family.
I pray for continued discernment between the things I need and those I want.
Most of all, keep me focused on You. Amen.

Nothin' Like a Little Frettin' with Your Coffee

"Fear not, for I am with you;
be not dismayed, for I am your God.
I will strengthen you, yes, I will help you,
I will uphold you with My righteous right hand."

ISAIAH 41:10 NKJV

I'm worried. There's a situation going on at work where it's my manager's word against mine. My employer's human resources department has gotten involved. What a mess!

I sip my coffee and stare at my Bible, which lay on the kitchen table.

They'll never believe me. They'll take her side over mine.

I run a finger along the edge of God's Word.

Lord, what am I going to do? How much of an issue should I make of this? Why didn't I see this trouble brewing?

I take another drink of coffee, wondering what I should eat for breakfast. After a few moments of deliberation, I get up from my chair at the table and prepare two boiled eggs and a piece of toast.

Thank You for this food, Lord.

As I eat, I think about the situation going on at work. I worry about the outcome. I sip my coffee and fret some more.

Lord, why can't I hear Your voice? I'm sitting here talking to You, and You're so quiet.

As if God tapped me on the shoulder, my attention is drawn to my Bible. I am prompted to open it up. As I flip through the delicate pages, I come to today's verse in the book of Isaiah, chapter 40. Suddenly I realized I've been having a monologue and not dialogue! No wonder I couldn't hear God.

"Fear not...I am with you.... Be not dismayed, for I am your God.... I will strengthen you...I will help you...."

My vision blurs with tears after reading my Savior's love letter to me. His Word is true; God cannot lie (Titus 1:2).

"I will uphold you with My righteous right hand." Thank You, Jesus.

Hours later, I walk into my manager's office and sit down. Nervous flutters fill my insides, but I hang on to what God promised.

"I talked with Human Resources." My manager squares her shoulders and folds her hands on her desk. "We found a discrepancy in your file. A correction will be made."

"So I was right?"

My manager hesitates before nodding in admission.

Relief washes over me. Minutes later, I leave her office, breathing a sigh of relief. *Wow, that was easy, Lord.*

His gentle rebuke fills my soul. *I told you not to fret. I've got you covered.*

Okay, no more frettin' with my coffee. From now on, I only fret to God. ✳ *AKB*

Today's Prayer

Lord, worry is a sin because You have said many times in Your Word not to fret or worry or be troubled or dismayed. Help me today to take my problems to You, Lord God, and to leave them at Your nail-pierced feet.

You already have the answers, because You have plotted out my future right to its end, to bring me good and not evil. I thank You, Lord, for hearing my prayers, for being the great Savior that You are. In Jesus' name, amen.

Practice Makes Perfect

Therefore submit to God.
Resist the devil and he will flee from you.
JAMES 4:7 NKJV

At one time in my life, I was going for long walks about five days a week. However, after a foot injury, I realized one day that it had been almost two months since I'd gone for a walk. Just hoofing it from the parking garage into my office set my heart to pounding and the rest of me to huffing and puffing. This was my body's way of telling me that it was time to lace up the walking shoes and get my fanny into gear!

So on Monday night, when the weather was cool and a soft breeze was blowing, I did just that. I was tired after only a fraction of the distance I could formerly walk, but I pressed on. At least I was moving again.

On Wednesday night, I went again. I couldn't rack up much more distance than the previous time, but I felt pretty good about following through with my Monday-Wednesday-Friday plan.

On Friday, though, my head was turned by an invitation to join a girlfriend at our favorite Mexican restaurant. And by the end of the weekend, my Monday-Wednesday-Friday plan had slipped from my mind and out the door without so much as a creak on the floorboards.

"So how's your walking schedule going?" I was asked a couple of weeks later.

"Oh, well, umm, not so great lately."

The truth was, I'd forgotten all about that schedule. With new resolve at the reminder, I hit the REFRESH button on my brain and decided to start anew. But after a week or so, the distractions won out.

"I don't know what my problem is," I heard someone say on a morning talk show. "I mean to get fit and stay active, but I just don't have the time."

The guest was a fitness trainer, and he explained the importance of keeping a routine for at least one full month. He purported that, after a certain amount of time of doing the same thing again and again, something clicks inside the brain and it becomes a habit—and for most people that span of time is a month.

I remembered when my neighbor quit smoking; she'd been told the same thing by her pastor. "Resist and keep resisting until the devil flees," the pastor had said. I supposed the same premise would hold true for forming good habits as well as destroying old ones.

Recently, when a girlfriend called on a Wednesday night to invite me to the movies, I sang, "Resisting you, devil! I'm going for a walk." Later, we laughed at the idea that by joining me for my walk rather than crunching buttered popcorn at the movies, she was doing a little resisting of her own. ✳ *SDB*

Today's Prayer

Thank You, Father, for Your Word that somehow applies to every corner of my life, in every situation. Help me to dig deep into scripture so that I can create for myself a reservoir of promises and reminders to keep Your grace alive in my heart. In Jesus' precious name I pray, amen.

Chocolate

Wherefore do ye spend money for that which is not bread?
and your labour for that which satisfieth not?
hearken diligently unto me, and eat ye that which is good,
and let your soul delight itself in fatness.

ISAIAH 55:2 KJV

Mel Gibson once said, "After about twenty years of marriage, I'm finally starting to scratch the surface of what women want, and I think the answer lies somewhere between conversation...and chocolate." (These days, I'll bet he and his wife wish he'd talked less...and bought more chocolate!) Still, the quote makes me wish politicians would draft a new law requiring every husband, boyfriend, father, brother, and son to recite Mel's quote at least once a year!

It's no secret that I love chocolate. Always have, always will. My first memory of the slippery-when-soft substance was the Easter before my fourth birthday, when Nonna hid Hershey's Kisses (my all-time-favorite form of the stuff) all around her cozy dining room. In no time, the cotton candy–pink dress I'd worn to church bore streaky evidence of my finds.

Nowadays, when my too-busy life threatens to overwhelm me, I'm assured a moment of calm and comfort...if I stop and spend a quiet moment unwrapping a Hershey's Kiss. I pop it onto my tongue and wait as it melts with deliberate, delicious slowness, spreading choco-joy throughout my mouth.

It's as I unwrap those foil-shrouded delights that I'm reminded how, all around me, God has provided sweet reminders...proof that life isn't just about work, deadlines, and racing around like a madwoman to cross every item off today's to-do list. He uses the lure of chocolate to force me to stop, and as I'm enjoying the delectable delicacies, I notice robins and finches splashing in the birdbath outside my window. I spy a bright new bud on one of my rosebushes. Or I catch the expression of unconditional love emanating from the furry face of my faithful mutt.

Without my tiny treats, would I notice meaningful lyrics lilting from the radio in my office? Would I acknowledge camera-captured images of my lovely daughters and their families, smiling from the shelf above my desk?

Probably.

But each moment is sweeter and lasts longer when I'm feasting on my favorite candy. As I toss wrappers into the trash, I'm acutely aware that God has used those moments to awaken my senses, broaden my imagination, and exercise my "thank you for the little things!" muscles.

Because there are days when not even the most soothing symphony can stir my soul the way chocolate can. The sweet treat is capable of turning me from a pessimist into an optimist who believes that if no one witnesses my consumption, the calories don't count. If I had proof that there's chocolate in heaven, would I try even harder to live by the Golden Rule!

I think I'll pop a handful of Kisses into my pocket, so I can say "God bless you!" and hand them out to the strangers I meet today! ✳ *LL*

Today's Prayer

Most heavenly Father, Your humble servant is so grateful for Your daily reminders that life's sweetness can sometimes be found in the tiniest of packages wrapped in thin squares of shiny foil. Oh, how great and mighty You are, to remind me that, sometimes, blessings and gifts are more obvious when I peer through the innocent eyes of a child! Amen.

What's Wrong with Being Jill the Admin?

*"Judge not, that you be not judged.
For with what judgment you judge, you will be judged;
and with the measure you use, it will be measured back to you."*

MATTHEW 7:1–2 NKJV

When I first entered college, I assumed it would be my golden ticket to the job of my dreams. Was I in for a surprise when I graduated! Not only did I get HR doors slammed in my face, I was told I wasn't qualified for anything other than a clerical position—something I could have done without a degree.

After I worked for a temp agency and eventually accepted an admin job, I got into the groove of my daily tasks. I learned that I actually enjoyed being someone's assistant. It enabled me to earn a living and then go home at the end of the day without worrying about work-related problems, unlike those higher on the corporate ladder.

Then one day I heard from a social service agency where I had applied for a director's position. They needed someone who could start right away, and I was next on their list of prospective candidates. After a couple of long interviews with the executive director and the board members, I was offered what I always thought I wanted. Since it was a social service agency, the pay was only so-so, but my title sounded good. People were impressed that someone so young could be in such a position. For a while I actually enjoyed my work—but mostly the prestige of the title.

My assistant was so good and vital to our programs that I leaned on her as much as she allowed, which was quite a bit. Occasionally someone would demand to speak to a supervisor, so she'd calmly put them through to me. That made me feel bad for her, so one day I asked her if she'd like a new title. The board of my agency was made up of an understanding group of women, so I was pretty sure they'd go along with my request. My assistant tilted her head, gave me a questioning look, and said, "Why? What's wrong with being an administrative assistant?"

Wow! What an eye-opener! And she was right! What was wrong with being an assistant? Every admin assistant I knew was smart, efficient, and respected.

Judging people by their title or pay range is wrong. A good administrative assistant is one of the most valuable people in any company. ✱ DM

Today's Prayer

Thank You, Lord, for people who understand their value. Please forgive those who are ignorant and judge people by their perception of what is important. I pray that You'll continue to remind me that all believers are loved by You and that our earthly title will have no significance in eternity. Amen.

Everyday Wisdom

And to man He said, "Behold, the fear of the Lord, that is wisdom,
and to depart from evil is understanding."

JOB 28:28 NKJV

A coworker tried to convince me why it was all right for her to live with her "fiancé," a man who wasn't a believer. It was none of my business, and I told her so, but she persisted to justify herself to me each time we went on a break at work. She considered herself my "sister in Christ," and, knowing I was a trained life coach, she trusted me. So I listened.

"Derek and me...well, we've made a commitment to each other. We were together before I became a Christian. It's like we're married. God knows my heart. We're married in His eyes."

In reply, I merely suggested that she read God's Word so she'd learn His heart, but my words seemed to fall on deaf ears.

As the days passed, I longed to share God's truth with her. I considered Lisa a friend. I wanted her to understand that living in a sexual relationship apart from marriage, while socially acceptable today, is by God's standards unacceptable. The Bible refers to it as "fornication." What's more, the Lord warns us in His Word that "no fornicator...has any inheritance in the kingdom of Christ and God" (Ephesians 5:5 NKJV). That's strong language—and I didn't think Lisa would appreciate my preaching to her, even though she sought out my opinions. I felt that God needed to speak to Lisa personally.

So I began to pray.

About a month later, she approached me and said that she and Derek had split. She'd been reading her Bible and began talking about God and the two of them going to church—even getting married. "For whatever reason," she told me, "Derek flipped out. He got really mad, said I was trying to trap him, and he threw stuff around our apartment. Then he packed up and left. He said he never wants to see me again."

I held my tongue but thought, *Good thing you didn't marry the jerk!* Instead, I asked, "So are you two really finished, or are you going to try to win him back?"

"Win him back?" Lisa laughed. "No way. He's history. I mean, I don't think he ever intended to marry me. He used me. I paid the rent and the bills, bought groceries, and made dinner. I cleaned the apartment and decorated it, and he sat back and sponged it all up...but all the while he allowed me to think we'd get married someday."

My heart broke for my friend, but at the same time I knew the breakup was for the best—her best. "I'm sorry you got hurt."

"Actually, I'm relieved. I'll never make that mistake again. I've learned that commitments go beyond mere words. The prerequisite for the next guy I date is that he has to be a serious Christian who plays by God's rules, and I'll have to see his faith in action to believe it. Know what I mean?"

I nodded. "I think so."

"I really care what God thinks. I want His blessing, not His curse."

Her reply was my answered prayer! Lisa now had a healthy fear and a solid respect for the Lord and His Word.

I smiled. "You're a wise woman, Lisa." ❋ *AKB*

Today's Prayer

Dearest heavenly Father, help us to see that today's modern ways of living aren't necessarily Your ways. Help us honor You in all we say and do. Help us to be ornaments of Your love, grace, and mercy so others will be drawn to You. In Christ's name we pray, amen.

The Meeting from You-Know-Where

"Therefore, brethren, having boldness to enter
the Holiest by the blood of Jesus,
by a new and living way which He consecrated for us,
through the veil, that is..."

HEBREWS 10:19–20 NKJV

I sat in the waiting room for forty-five minutes before the receptionist finally called me over to her desk.

"I'm so sorry," she said, "but Mr. Devlin isn't going to be able to see you today after all."

I'd phoned ahead and waited for more than six weeks for this appointment. I was fully prepared with a marketing plan and references from other similar corporate types with whom we'd done business. I knew Devlin was in his office because everyone could hear him on the phone, shouting about some deal gone wrong, and he'd kept me waiting for forty-five minutes beyond our appointment time, during which he'd had his lunch delivered. Now he couldn't see me?

"I don't think so," I replied softly.

"Pardon me?"

"I said, I don't think so."

Recounting the bumps in the road leading up to that moment, I explained that I didn't need more than ten minutes of his time and respectfully told the receptionist that I would appreciate it if she would ask him again. She did, and I got the meeting I'd been waiting for. I was even able to strike a deal on behalf of my most important client within the first ten minutes in Devlin's office. When we parted, he told me he admired my tenacity.

I'd done everything right in setting up the meeting with this very elusive businessman, and now it was up to him to do the right thing. When it looked as if he wasn't going to follow through, I punched right through the outer veil with boldness (as well as courtesy), and it paid off.

Why is it that we are often so timid about taking our challenges and petitions to the throne of our Lord? He's done everything right to provide us the privilege of doing so, and yet we hesitate.

The cleansing blood of Jesus Christ has washed the pathway before us, making straight a road that was once very crooked, and a loving Savior awaits, hoping for the opportunity to bless us in some way. So may we consistently be reminded that the way has been consecrated for us.

Enter in, beyond the veil, with boldness and thanksgiving! ✳ *SDB*

Today's Prayer

Thank You for being a Lord who makes crooked roads straight. I love You for giving me the confidence and authority to boldly enter Your throne room, and for giving me the assurance that You are a Father who eagerly awaits my arrival there. In the holy name of my Savior, Jesus, I pray, amen.

Let My Mirror Reflect Joy

One dieth in his full strength, being wholly at ease and quiet...
and another dieth in the bitterness of his soul....

JOB 21:23, 25 KJV

I've struggled recently, trying to figure out how to deal with a person whose behavior makes it pretty clear that she resents me. Petty comments—made privately and in public—not only deeply hurt my feelings but cause discomfort for innocent bystanders who are subjected to her anger.

It doesn't matter, really, whether she's doing it on purpose. What matters is...it's starting to make *me* feel resentful.

And therein, as Shakespeare so astutely said, lies the rub.

Because every time I think I've beat back my vexation with self-pep talks like "Get over yourself!"or "Focus on other things" or "Let it *go*," she fires another volley to remind me just how much she doesn't like me.

The problem has driven me to my knees a dozen times, where I tearfully pray to understand the *why* of it and beseech the Lord to fortify me with the strength of character to not succumb to resentment myself.

But it's tough, letting go of the hurt, when I'm surrounded by reminders of her resentment. Just this morning, in an e-mail written to a list of recipients, came another snarky barb...and, behind it, the "grin" emoticon, to disguise its true meaning and intent.

Like children calling, "Tag, you're it!" her resentment sparked mine. Again. And because I hate that feeling (and the weakness that inspires it), I hit my knees. Again. And glory of glories, the Lord reminded me that the Good Book has plenty to say about resentment!

It's a waste of time, for starters—time I could put to better use by serving Him. As Job 5:2 so aptly puts it, worrying over resentment is a foolish, useless emotion, since mirroring her resentment with more of my own only hurts me...and those the Lord has put me here to love and serve.

It came into my head that telling God how much her resentment hurts me isn't enough. I have to let down my guard and admit that, in my weakness, I'm tempted to resent her right back!

It also dawned on me that psychiatrists have a lot to say about resentment, too. Studies prove that, most times, it's deeply rooted in envy. I have absolutely no idea why she's jealous of me! But the idea that she *might* be struck a nerve, making me realize that if that's the explanation behind her mean-spirited behavior, she's suffering far more than I am! The very idea awakened protective feelings toward her, and my prayers instantly turned from "Help *me*, Lord!" to "Show me how I can help *her*!"

I believe in my heart that when her next carefully disguised emoticon punctuates a spiteful jab, it isn't going to hurt at all. ✳ *LL*

Today's Prayer

Lord Father, I thank You for covering my so-called wounds with the balm of Your healing mercy. Thank You for showing me how to behave with compassion and forgiveness instead of bitterness and resentment. Thank You for teaching me that only by letting go of such childish feelings can I grasp Your gentle and peaceful attitude. And thank You, O Jesus, for reminding me of these things every day of my life! Amen.

The Rock-Star Life

...that you also aspire to lead a quiet life, to mind your own business,
and to work with your own hands, as we commanded you....

1 Thessalonians 4:11 NKJV

As I sit here on a Saturday night, typing this devotion, I'm thinking about how unexciting my life is. Paris Hilton and Jessica Simpson would be bored to tears, but I'm actually very content. While they're bar-crawling and party-hopping, I'm sitting at the kitchen table in my daughter and son-in-law's house, praying every few minutes for my little granddaughter's jaundice to go away. Someone more exciting from the world's view might feel sorry for me, but the simple life suits me just fine.

Don't get me wrong. There are some aspects to the rock-star life that appeal to me. I enjoy travel, interesting people, designer handbags, and great food. An occasional party is fun, too, but I need to be home by midnight or my brain turns to pie filling.

Mick Jagger sings, "You can't always get what you want." That's a good thing in my book. If I had everything I wanted, I also wouldn't ever be *satisfied*, another theme of one of his songs. Hmm. Perhaps Mick knows more than he lets on.

A rock star's life appears exciting on the surface. However, if you think about it, they have their own routines and mundane tasks. While touring, they spend most of their days on tour buses. Then they get on stages that basically all look alike, playing to crowds who shout and scream the same things. When they're home, they fall back into another routine. Even if it's partying all night, it's still a routine. The one thing that sets a rock star apart from the real world is that they depend on other people's attention.

Obviously, I don't live a rock-star life. My days are spent doing peaceful, mundane tasks that I've learned to appreciate over the years.

First thing each morning, I sip my coffee and reflect on God's Word before I turn my thoughts to what I need to do that day. Once in a while, I shake things up and have lunch with friends or speak to groups who think I have something interesting to say about writing. But for the most part, my life wouldn't suit a rock star who needs constant adulation and thrills. I feel that I'm just as blessed as they are, but in a much deeper, more real way. What I have can't be dashed by fans who have turned their attention elsewhere. My faith in Christ gives me more of a rush than standing before thousands of screaming fans. ✳ DM

Today's Prayer

Thank You, Jesus, for the peace in my life. I know that too much excitement can lead to highs and lows that bring despair and dissatisfaction, while You're a constant force providing hope for anyone who believes in You. Whenever I feel the urge for more thrills, give me a gentle nudge to remind me to settle down. Amen.

She Done Him *Way* Wrong

But as for you,
you meant evil against me;
but God meant it for good.
GENESIS 50:20 NKJV

I can't imagine how Joseph felt when his jealous brothers sold him into slavery. Then his situation went from bad to worse when Potiphar's wife (Joseph's master's wife) tried to seduce him. Joseph refused, saying, "How then can I do this great wickedness, and sin against God?" (Genesis 39:9 NKJV). The woman was angered that she couldn't persuade him to sleep with her and, in spite, told her husband that Joseph attempted to rape her. Joseph was sent to prison (Genesis 39:10–20).

At the end of this biblical account, Joseph was reunited with his brothers, who begged his forgiveness. Joseph (a powerful man at that time) didn't order them to be publicly flogged, although he could have. Rather, Joseph forgave his brothers, saying, "You meant evil against me; but God meant it for good" (Genesis 50:20 NKJV).

Mind-blowing, isn't it? Divine forgiveness versus human nature's desire to retaliate? That's not to say that forgiveness always comes with a snap of two fingers. Many times forgiveness is a process, depending, of course, on the nature of the circumstance.

In her book *Counseling through Your Bible Handbook*, June Hunt writes that there are four stages to forgiveness:

1) Face the Offense: "You must face the truth of what actually happened...."
2) Feel the Offense: "Anger or even hatred toward an offender needs to be brought up out of the basement of our souls and dealt with."

3) Forgive the Offender: "You are called by God to forgive" (see Mark 11:25).
4) Find Oneness when Appropriate: "Relationships filled with resentment ultimately perish, while relationships filled with forgiveness ultimately prevail."

Did you ever ask, "How could she take him back?" or "How could he forgive her?" Well, forgiveness is an act of will powered by God's Word. It's how wives can forgive unfaithful husbands and vice versa. It's how adult children can forgive their abusive parents. This is how friends can forgive one another.

And with true forgiveness comes healing, followed by freedom, joy, peace, and most of all, the goodness of God! ✳ *AKB*

Today's Prayer

Dear God, thank You for caring about me and the world of hurt
that hides in my soul. Set it free, Lord, and help me face it. It's painful.
But I forgive the person who put it there. I now lift the weight of hurt, anger,
and guilt off my shoulders and put it onto Yours because You are God,
and You can carry the heavy load. I praise You for the freedom that
forgiveness brings, and I look forward to the miraculous things
You are about to do in my life.

Counseling through Your Bible Handbook by June Hunt was published by Harvest House Publishers in 2008. Selections taken from pages 186–188.

Flying Under the Radar

A thousand may fall at your side,
and ten thousand at your right hand;
but it shall not come near you.

PSALM 91:7 NKJV

Have you ever heard the old adage, "You don't know what you've got till it's gone"? Well, I'd worked at a particular company for three years, and despite the fact that I was deeply grateful for the job, I was never particularly fond of it. Over time, it became more and more challenging to think of new ways to motivate myself to keep at it. And then one day the rumor we'd been hearing for several months was standing at the door waiting for us when we clocked in. The Tampa office would be closing in just sixty days.

I'd been praying that this wouldn't happen, citing God's scriptural promise that ten thousand might fall right beside me but it wouldn't come near me. However, it had not only come near me but I'd been slapped by the reality of just what I dreaded the most: unemployment.

As those first days wore on, I started recognizing clear patterns among my coworkers. Many of them began making plans to live off their severance for as long as possible for a little paid vacation; others decided unemployment benefits would get them by and the severance funds would be better used toward a new stereo system or computer. Others, like me, started preparing for job hunting within the first hours after the news.

Because I'd been miserable in my line of work for three years, I immediately began to wonder about changing fields. I redesigned my resume and collected letters of recommendation that targeted a new direction, and I applied for a "dream job," one that appealed to me more than any of the others on the job boards. You can imagine my surprise when that very job, the first one for which I'd applied, was the first offer I received.

Weeks passed, and the mood in the office began to change. A sense of desperation ensued and then panic that seemed to permeate every conversation between coworkers. Because I already had something to go to, I was able to relax and comfort my friends, even help them by redesigning their resumes and making suggestions about how to target jobs that might be a good fit for them.

On the day that the doors closed at our company for the final time, one of my coworkers gave me a hug and thanked me for helping her through those last days.

"It was encouraging to watch you," she commented. "It was like everything was falling around you but it didn't touch you at all."

My prayers and that foundational scripture sprang to mind, and I grinned at her. "Thank you," I said. "You just reminded me who is really in charge here."

The Lord knew all along that the company was going to close. He knew that I would be looking for a change, and He prepared the ground ahead of me so that I could survive the thousand falling at my side. He walked me right through so that I would be in a position to be a blessing to those around me. ✳ *SDB*

Today's Prayer

Why do I so easily forget that You have me in the palm of Your large and loving hand, Lord? Thank You so much for teaching me, time after time, that Your ways and thoughts are much higher than mine. Help me today to stand firm in that grace and love so I can bring comfort to others and shine the light of Your love to illuminate their way. Use me, Lord Jesus, to be a blessing to those around me each time You shield me from the raging battle. In Your holy and loving name, I pray, amen.

You Are What You Think

*Therefore I say unto you, what things soever ye desire,
when ye pray, believe that ye receive them, and ye shall have them.*

MARK 11:24 KJV

A pessimist, it's said, sees the difficulty in opportunity, while an optimist sees opportunity in every difficulty. Oh, that we could all think like optimists all the time! Our thoughts, much too often, turn into words. And if what we're thinking is negative stuff, we're bound to say things that will turn others' smiles upside down, in addition to our own.

What we see and hear—and how we react to it—is directly connected to everything we are and do. For centuries, the sages have said that the tongue is the most difficult part of the body to control. The Bible has a lot to say about this human peculiarity. It strongly urges believers to renew their minds and change their attitudes to ensure that their actions are as upbeat as the rest of their lives.

Some mind-body experts have compared the "mind over matter" dilemma to medical studies that separate pill-testing patients into two groups: One group receives the real thing while the other gets a placebo, but neither is told which is which. Doctors dole out pills along with a list of possible side effects, and they're always amazed at the results, because the fake stuff can cause drowsiness, nausea, palpitations, headaches, and vomiting...just like the actual medication. Just as amazingly, every miserable symptom disappears the instant patients stop taking the placebo!

Positive thinking, they say, is a very real and powerful thing. And guess what? It's every bit as contagious as the illnesses, diseases, and disorders those researchers are trying to cure by comparing real meds to placebos.

So the next time you wake up in a truly bummy mood, remember that your attitude is not something you must accept. Nor do you have to allow it to shadow you for the entire day. And it needn't invade your conversation and relationships as you go about your business, either.

The Swiss have a great attitude about attitude. "Fear less, hope more; eat less, chew more; whine less, breathe more; talk less, say more; love more, and good things will be yours." Some might say that's a tad cheesy, but I say there are no "holes" in that quote!

Bottom line? If you ask the Lord to blanket you with happy thoughts and an upbeat mind-set, that's exactly what you'll get.

And on those days when it seems you just can't shake that bad mood, remember what the comedian/philosopher Herm Albright said: "A positive attitude might not solve all your problems, but it will annoy enough people to make it worth the effort." ✳ *LL*

Today's Prayer

O Father, anoint me with a joyful heart, so that as I move about in the world,
I will be a shining example of how a deep and abiding relationship with You
can turn a weak human into a strong Christian. Amen!

My Secret

"Indeed He says, 'It is too small a thing that You should be My Servant to raise up the tribes of Jacob, and to restore the preserved ones of Israel; I will also give You as a light to the Gentiles, that You should be My salvation to the ends of the earth.'"

ISAIAH 49:6 NKJV

*B*ack when I was in college, I worked at a health club that had quite a few wealthy members. I was one of a half-dozen exercise and fitness instructors who catered to folks with maids, gardeners, and assorted other servants at home. I often thought about how nice it would be to walk in their shoes, and I dreamed of the day when I would graduate, find a high-paying job, and live the life I assumed my clients led. (Although my boss told me that I'd never make a lot of money doing what I did, but I'd find some satisfaction from helping others.)

A couple of years after I started, one of my favorite clients invited me to lunch. My boss gave me the go-ahead (I didn't want to do anything unethical), so I accepted. I was excited to have even a slight taste of this woman's endlessly glorious life. But I was shocked to learn that she was miserable.

We spent the first half hour ordering and chatting about mostly insignificant things. Then she fidgeted for a moment, gulped, and reached out her hand. "Debby," she said softly, "what's your secret?"

I tilted my head and gave her one of those clueless looks. *What secret?*

"You always seem so happy. I never see you without a smile. I want what you have."

I was stunned into silence. She wanted what I had?

"But you have everything you could possibly want," I squeaked.

A smile slowly crept over her face as she shook her head. "It might look that way, but I'm miserable. I spend most of my days trying to fight depression. I go to the health club every day hoping that some of your joy will rub off on me."

That was a major eye-opener. I really was a happy person, and it certainly wasn't because I had a lot of external things to keep me that way. Between tight quarters in my dorm room and a car that I prayed would start every time I got in it, there was always something that could be improved.

My joy came from within—that feeling of knowing Christ was always with me. I wasn't sure how I'd be received, but I took a chance and told my client the source of my happiness. To my surprise, she teared up and said, "I thought that might be the case, but I wasn't sure. I haven't been to church in years. Do you think it would be okay if I went sometime? With you?"

Of course I said I would love it! ✲ DM

Today's Prayer

Lord Jesus, I pray that You'll keep me content with a servant's heart. Fill me with confidence to accept where I am, and give me opportunities to share the good news with others. Amen.

Broken Things

"For God did not send His Son into the world to condemn the world, but that the world through Him might be saved."

JOHN 3:17 NKJV

I have watched with a saddened heart as several Christians gave up on their faith. They stumbled in their walks, got lost in the darkness, and figured there was no way back to Jesus. Worse, they believed that God didn't want them back because of their blemished pasts. After all, friends and family—even former church family members—didn't want them back.

But the truth is, God will take us and our hurtful pasts and use them all together for His good (Romans 8:28). Of course, repentance is involved with restoration. But if we confess our sins, He is faithful and just to forgive us and cleanse us from all unrighteousness (1 John 1:9). Once restored, our hearts can't even condemn us, because God is greater than our guilt-ridden, broken hearts.

This magnificent truth in no way gives us a license to sin, but I have seen God take the pieces of a broken life, put them back together, and create a thing of extraordinary beauty—and one that's of great service to Him.

God really does use broken things. * AKB

Today's Prayer

Father God, so many people stand in condemnation of us and others, but that's not what You stand for. You're the Giver of Life. You are Love, and You came so that we can live more abundantly. We thank You, we praise and worship You, and we rejoice in the miracles You're about to do in our lives. In Jesus' precious name, amen.

Times Not Meant for the Faint of Heart

"Do not fear, for you will not be ashamed;
neither be disgraced, for you will not be put to shame;
for you will forget the shame of your youth,
and will not remember the reproach of your widowhood anymore.
For your Maker is your husband, the LORD of hosts is His name;
and your Redeemer is the Holy One of Israel;
He is called the God of the whole earth."

ISAIAH 54:4–5 NKJV

I was sixteen when I met Marian for the first time. She was a couple of years older than I was, a barrel of fun, and so pretty. All the boys' heads turned when Marian walked across a room, and I felt *cooler* just being around her. We've been through some roller coaster years together, but now, at fifty-*cough* years old, Marian is still one of my favorite people. She still turns heads, she can still make me laugh in a nanosecond, and I still feel a little bit cooler just by being in her company.

When I met Stan for the first time, I remember scratching my head. This wasn't the husband I had pictured for Marian! He was a cowboy, and she was a social butterfly. But over the many years since they'd found one another, I was able to get to know him better—his humor, his wit, his enormous heart—and I started to see the beauty in the pairing. It simply worked for them.

Stan died on my birthday this year. I was heartbroken not just at losing him, but in knowing that, for the rest of her life, my dearest friend would remember my birthday as the day she lost her partner in life.

I expected her to fall apart; after all, that's what I did when my first love died. I closed myself away from everyone who loved me, rejecting any offered comfort, reminding myself several dozen times a day that I would never love anyone like that again and no one would ever love me. But Marian's strength and grace in the absolute worst of times, and her ability to take such joy in the memory of her dear husband as she simultaneously dealt with his loss, was astonishing.

I'd watched her faith blossom over the decades that we'd known each other, but it occurred to me on the morning of Stan's memorial service that, rather than losing herself in fears about the future or misgivings about how to live without her husband, Marian was leaning hard on the God she knew she could rely upon. She knew that secret only believers know; she was held up by the promise that her Maker was her husband now.

Times such as these are not recommended to the faint of heart; however, with deep and abiding faith also comes strength. And wearing the godly strength that she's grown into makes me feel far more secure— and just a little bit *cooler!*—when basking in the illuminated light of my friend's faith. ✳ *SDB*

Today's Prayer

Thank You, Lord, for being my Maker and my Husband. Whether I am single or married, a professional or a homemaker, it is Your hand that guides me, Your provision that sustains me. Help me to remember that each day is another step through life with You at my side.

You Are What You Say (and Do)

And as ye would that men should do to you,
do ye also to them likewise.

LUKE 6:31 KJV

You've heard it said that reputation is what others think you are, but character is *who* you are.

Two of my favorite quotes come to mind when mulling over that one.

The first is the one my grandfather quoted when one of us grabbed a cookie before dinner, crossed the street without looking both ways, or snooped in his attic without permission...and stretched the truth when he caught us red-handed at any of those things:

"Your thoughts," he'd say, pointing at each of us in turn, "become words. Words become actions. Actions become character. And character is everything."

I don't imagine any of his little cookie thieves knew what in the world he was talking about...until we grew older and spent some serious time in the real world. Then the hazy meaning of the adage became clearer, and we began to understand that it's synonymous with my other favorite, the Golden Rule.

"Do unto others as you'd have them do unto you" has long been the center point for morality, ethics, religion, and politics. It's the worldwide litmus test for fairness and decency. And Matthew and Luke weren't the only Bible scholars who believed in the concept. Quite the contrary! Mark, John, James, Paul, and Jonah cited it, and similar passages can be found in Proverbs, Leviticus, Deuteronomy, and others, as well.

More than twenty world religions have adopted some version of its intent and meaning as doctrine. Confucius touted it as a moral truth, and in 1963, President Kennedy reminded citizens of its intent in an anti-segregation speech. "The heart of the question," he said, "is whether we are going to treat our fellow Americans the way we want to be treated." To apply it, we must first try to identify with our brothers and sisters and, as my American Indian ancestors would have said, be willing to walk a mile in their moccasins.

I try to remember these famous sage-isms when a driver cuts me off in traffic, people at the grocery store dump whole cartloads of merchandise on the conveyor belt in the Fifteen Items or Less line, or someone says something to hurt my feelings. Instead of an in-kind knee-jerk reaction, I recite Luke 6:31 and Grandpa's maxim, too.

Because I hope that by living by the Golden Rule, my reputation as a woman of Christian character will precede me...and follow me... everywhere. ✳ LL

Today's Prayer

Jesus, Lord and Savior, continue to teach me the true meaning of turning the other cheek. Let the life I lead prove to the world that a Christian's heart becomes caring and forgiving through the strength found in Your Word.

Nothing Ventured

The generous soul will be made rich,
and he who waters will also be watered himself.

PROVERBS 11:25 NKJV

"What do you get out of that?" "Why should I bother with him? What did he ever do for me?"

These are questions people often ask when they feel imposed upon to do something nice for someone else. But what else can we expect with the self-focused lives we lead? From commercials that try to convince us we "deserve" something merely because we exist to the common mantra "If it feels good, then it must be right."

Ever since I became an adult, I've worked hard. I'm also somewhat of a risk taker, evidenced by the fact that I resigned from my full-time job to be a freelance writer and teacher. I feel like I need to try new things—but I have to admit, most of my risks are well-thought-out and taken only after I've worked through the downside in my mind...and feel confident that I can live with it.

I also enjoy doing community service. One of the things I love about working on my own is making my own hours so I can choose when and where to volunteer. And I know the place I should go.

In my last job, we were encouraged to spend two days per year "volunteering," which is a misnomer since the company paid us for our time. The most difficult yet rewarding day for me was when I helped out at the local food bank. At home, the very thought of reorganizing shelves and putting everything in order sends a shiver of dread down my spine. However, knowing that organization was critical to feed the masses made it tolerable. All morning I worked with about twenty other volunteers, pulling apart sacks and putting canned beans in the bean boxes and hams in the canned meat boxes. That afternoon, they split us into groups: some to distribute the food, some to work in the toy room, and others to interview clients. I went with the last group.

As I spoke to each person who needed food, I realized how richly blessed I was for being able to do this. My venture into this world of need gave me a new perspective. Now if I see a food bank bin when I shop for groceries, I often purchase something to put in there. It feels wonderful to do something for someone else—even though I don't know the people who will be on the receiving end. The Lord has blessed me by allowing me to feed and clothe my family. But He's blessed me even more by allowing me to help others. My true gain is much greater than theirs. ✹ DM

Today's Prayer

Thank You, heavenly Father, for continuing to bless me
and allowing me to help others. Amen.

Pulling Down Strongholds

*For the weapons of our warfare are not carnal
but mighty in God for pulling down strongholds.*

2 CORINTHIANS 10:4 NKJV

I believe that God uses the hidden things of life to bring us to Him (or closer to Him) and to pull down our strongholds.

About thirteen years ago, shortly after I became a Christian, I received a phone call from a man who wanted to help with the foreclosure of our home. Soon I discovered that my husband, Daniel, had been gambling away the mortgage money for months—and I didn't have a clue. My husband was also an alcoholic. I doubted my marriage would last. I worried what would happen to my three young sons.

On my knees, pouring out my heart to God, I prayed that He would change my husband. Instead of changing my husband, God worked on me! As I prayed and prayed and worked at becoming a godly wife, my husband soon made decisions that honored Christ, which, in turn, changed his life and ours.

Today, Daniel is free from the bondages of alcohol and gambling. Jesus Christ set him free and pulled down those strongholds. Our sons saw the power of God in their father, which increased their faith.

Prayer is a mighty weapon that God uses to eliminate strongholds in our lives and the lives of those we care about. ✳ AKB

Today's Prayer

Lord, You said that the truth would set us free—Your truth. We'll watch
and rejoice when the strongholds in our lives come tumbling down.

Sticks and Stones

*Death and life are in the
power of the tongue.*
PROVERBS 18:21 NKJV

Sticks and stones may break my bones, but names will never hurt me."

When backed up with solid belief, this old adage is true. However, the sting of certain names can stay with us for our entire lives if we let it. Every time an accusation is hurled at us and we allow ourselves to ponder the authenticity of the label, we're building up a solid agreement to it, like adding stones to a foundational wall.

I've heard it said that children take on the role within their family that they most easily fit into. In my case, I was raised with an older brother who was an academic genius. He knew from a very young age that he was going to be a scientist of some kind, and everything he did revolved around his academic pursuits. My grades could never compete, so the role of Brainiac was taken. Who was I going to be?

My brother and his friends started early with the references to my being the "slow sister" and the one who could never keep up. By the time I was in junior high, they'd nicknamed me "Flash," and much of my persona was wrapped up in being the wide-eyed, naive little sister of that brilliant science student. It became who I was. I even sometimes wore the black T-shirt they'd given me for Christmas that had a silver glitter thunderbolt across it reading FLASH! On the off chance that I knew the answer to a science question in class, I almost never let on. By the time I reached college, I'd learned how to master the persona I'd adopted over those years. But it was by no means an indication of who I really was.

I was fortunate enough to meet and fall in love with a man who recognized someone smarter hiding behind the thunderbolt, and he was having no part in continuing to build upon it. He was the first one to point out to me the importance of realizing that we can create either death or life by the words we speak, and he taught me that we are easily snared by the words of our mouth. When I would make a joke at my own expense, he would speak to it with encouragement, canceling it out with truth.

If I hadn't had this amazing man come into my life at such a young age, there's no telling who I would have turned out to be. Perhaps, like some of my friends over the years, I'd have taken on the role of The Diva, The Athlete, or The Rebel and never discovered who I really was at the very core: *The Creative Spirit*.

Writing is a lifeline to me in my adult life. Telling a story, turning a phrase, finding a way to say something that will inspire others...these are the life's blood of who I really am. I might never have found this road if I'd allowed those early seeds to blossom and continue to take root.

So when children tell me they can't do something, I always try to be the one to tell them that, yes, they can. If they can't figure something out, I remind them that there's always another way to look at it. If they insinuate that they are ignorant or afraid or inept, I counteract those words with truth, the way my first love did for me.

And every morning, I begin by reminding myself, "If life and death are in the power of the tongue, I choose to speak *life* over my body, soul, spirit, and surroundings." ✳ *SDB*

Today's Prayer

Thank You so much, Lord Jesus, for Your daily reminders that I am a child of the Most High God, that I am unique and special, that I am the apple of my Father's eye, and that I have everything I need to fulfill my destiny. Help me to pass those reminders on to others in some way, each and every day, so that they might realize the joy of knowing life rather than death.

Little Mary

Give, and it shall be given unto you;
good measure, pressed down, and shaken together,
and running over, shall men give into your bosom.
For with the same measure that ye mete withal
it shall be measured to you again.

LUKE 6:38 KJV

It's been said that I should have been born a century ago, mostly because I'm so fond of the Wild West and its cowboys. In all honesty, I'm quite content with paved roads, electronic gadgets, and the miracles of modern medicine. It's the simple, straightforward way of the cowboy that I so admire, along with the down-to-earth terms they used to describe every element of life.

Take, for example, the term "Little Mary," the name given the fellow charged with driving the blatting cart—a vehicle designed to carry newborn calves unable to keep up with the herd. The guy holding the reins probably wasn't always tickled pink at his title, but he took it on the chin, knowing that someone had to look out for those babies.

Cowboy life often mirrored biblical principles. Those rowdy, dusty trail riders could have adopted a "survival of the fittest" mind-set, sparing the Little Mary driver's ego...and an equine team the grueling job of pulling the wagon. Instead, the cowboys looked to the future, knowing that every day the newborns grew more steady-legged and that by the time they reached the end of the trail, most of the calves would have the strength to stand on their own and keep up with the herd. So the riders outfitted the rig and turned a deaf ear to the chronic "blatting" of the young'uns, who were terrified by the rough ride that separated them from their mamas.

Cynics might say the efforts could be explained by a stoic realization that, eventually, each calf would deliver dollars by the pound. But that doesn't explain why the crusty cowpokes tenderly loaded and off-loaded critters hardly bigger than my clumsy dog at the start and finish of every parching day. Or why they crooned soft and low to calm them as the moon rose in the vast and inky sky. Or why those dog-tired men painstakingly fashioned "bottles" of leather gloves and hand-fed those li'l calves whose mothers couldn't—or wouldn't—provide nourishing milk and affection.

I believe we can all benefit by their example. The next time I see a brother or sister in need, I'll study them hard to find out what I can do to soothe them.

Fortunately for me, I won't have to bear the Little Mary moniker or clomp around on "yelpin' puppies," blistered and chafed by the grit and heat of a long, hard ride. Lucky me...I can ease on over and deliver comfort on well-padded Reeboks! ✳ *LL*

Today's Prayer

Lord Jesus, no matter how tired You were, You saw to the needs of others.
No one remained sick or lame or poor for very long in Your presence!
Teach me to have a sympathetic heart, so that I will recognize a need
when I see it. And grant me the loving-kindness to meet
those needs as best I can. Amen.

A Taste of Heaven

And my soul shall be joyful in the LORD;
it shall rejoice in His salvation.

PSALM 35:9 NKJV

I've had some of the most annoying frustrations lately. It would be easy to blame something or someone other than myself, but deep down, I know that my circumstances are no one else's fault. We just have to take that roller-coaster dip before we soar to the highest part of the track.

Some days, everything seems to go wrong. You forgot to set the alarm clock, so you're late for work. Then you get in the car and realize that you forgot to get gas on your way home the day before, so you have to stop, making you even later. When you get to the office, you discover that everyone's in the meeting room waiting for you because [gasp!] you're the one in charge of refreshments. And guess what? You're empty-handed.

If that's not enough to put a scowl on your face, I don't know what is. However, God calls us to be joyful, and He doesn't qualify it by saying "only when things are going well" or "only when you're in church." The deepest joy isn't something that circumstances can change; it only comes from knowing Christ.

I always got joy from my children—particularly when they were obedient...or sleeping. However, they were often determined to test my patience and faith that the Lord was always with me. At times I had to stop, turn my attention toward God, and ask for His guidance in how to handle a temper tantrum or for strength to say no to a heartfelt request, without losing my joy or making my children think I didn't find pleasure in having them with me all the time.

Sometimes we can't help but smile because everything is going so well. We feel happy when we have a wonderful meal of our favorite foods in front of us. It's delightful to have the means to take the family on a relaxing vacation. And we can be downright ecstatic when we drive off the car lot in a shiny new automobile. But that's not the joy God is talking about in this verse. He wants our joy to be deeper than anything the world can affect. He wants us to feel joy in knowing that He's our salvation. He wants what is best for our souls.

Have you ever met someone who puts on a happy face when they walk into church yet frown the second they leave the building? That person knows about the joy we only get from Christ, but she allows the world to zap it to misery because she reserves her "tastes of heaven" for that hour of Sunday morning worship.

Joy is always with us through the love of Christ and His promises of eternal life with Him. ✳ ᴰᴹ

Today's Prayer

It's so difficult, especially during trying times, to focus on Your Word.
I vow, dear Lord, to take my eyes off the world so I can experience
the joy of Your salvation. Amen.

I Quit!

"My sheep hear My voice, and I know them,
and they follow Me. And I give them eternal life, and they shall never perish;
neither shall anyone snatch them out of My hand."
JOHN 10:27–28 NKJV

Oh, it's no use. Just forget it. Why do I bother? Nobody cares....
Discouragement: The state of being deprived of confidence and courage. Like an ugly weed in a beautiful flower garden, discouragement can creep into our lives and choke our happiness. I've been there. I'm sure you have, too.

So how does one kill this wicked vine called discouragement? As a life coach, I teach three basic principles to begin the process:

1) Take your eyes off yourself and your situation.

In his best-selling book *The Purpose-Driven Life*, Rick Warren writes, "It's not about you. The purpose of your life is far greater than your own personal fulfillment, your peace of mind, or even your happiness. It's far greater than your family, your career, or even your wildest dreams and ambitions. If you want to know why you were placed on this planet, you must begin with God. You were born by His purpose and for His purpose."

Jesus Christ gave us eternal life, and no one can ever take that away from us. That truth alone ought to make us smile all day long. Even more incredible is to think that God created us to fulfill His divine plan. Focusing on Him will make the problems of the day seem like pebbles, not giant boulders that cannot be moved.

2) Read the Bible.

God's Word is very applicable for today's world and life's issues. Return to the Word Ministries states the following on its Web site, www.returntotheword.org: "The truths of God's Word [have] effectively shown the way for believers for thousands of years. More than ever, this generation needs to turn again to God Almighty for the answers to life's questions."

In essence, God's Word sets believers straight in their day-to-day attitudes and thought patterns. Without God's guidance, via His Word, believers are vulnerable to humanistic worldviews—after all, we are all human. But we need the divine!

3) Be a blessing to others.

Helping others can vaporize discouragement. Try assisting a stressed coworker even if it's not your job to do so, or help the elderly woman next door carry in her groceries.

Jesus, the Good Shepherd, said that His sheep (Christians) hear His voice and follow Him. A tall order, since our Savior led a selfless life. But with the Holy Spirit's help, we can accomplish His will. And while there may be no monetary reward in going out of our way for others, there is a spiritual one.... It's called joy. ✱ *AKB*

Today's Prayer

Heavenly Father, help me to look outside myself today. Help me to see beyond myself and lend a hand to someone else in need. Let me feel Your presence and Your love. In Jesus' name, I pray, amen.

The Purpose-Driven Life by Rick Warren was published by Zondervan in 2007 (paperback version). Selection taken from page 11.

Karaoke Isn't All Bad

*My people are destroyed
for lack of knowledge.*
Hosea 4:6 NKJV

I saw a news story recently about a four-year-old who was home alone with his mother. She was performing daily chores like laundry and dinner, doing all the things she did every day at that time. But she had the misfortune of taking one little misstep, and she fell all the way down a flight of stairs. The little boy knelt at her side, calling out to her, but she was unconscious. And Daddy wasn't due home for hours yet.

The headlines reporting this news story could have been horrific: "Young Boy Watches as Mom Dies" or "Child Traumatized by Mother's Household Accident."

Instead, one innocent little educational game the boy's mom had played with him the week prior changed the whole outcome of a terrible situation. She'd taught her young son his address...in a song.

Because Mom knew the value of her son having his personal information available, she'd made up a song about what to do in an emergency and how to tell authorities where he lived. The little boy knew to pick up her cell phone and dial 911, and then he sang the song again and again until the operator on the other end of the line was able to dispatch emergency technicians to the home.

When she'd taught the little boy his address, Mom had done it with the thought in mind that if anyone ever snatched him away from her, he could tell someone where he lived. Never once did she imagine he would be using that information to save her own life.

As I watched the news program, I thought about how there really aren't any coincidences in a life that follows after God. One little song taught to a four-year-old, for whatever reason, was the catalyst to save a life. The Word of God provides an instructional life for the reader. Seemingly insignificant tidbits and golden nuggets of information are imparted upon the Christian believer in verse after verse.

And then one day something occurs. A loved one is sick; a parent dies; a job is lost; or a home is foreclosed upon. At those times, reaching into our pocket and producing one of those golden nuggets to hang onto is going to make all the difference, just the way that address song changed the course of a young mother's life.

I'm reminded of a Sunday school song I used to sing with my students: "Greater is He that is in me; greater is He that is in me; greater is He that is in me than he that is in the world."

I'm humming that song more often these days...just in case I need a sudden reminder. ✳ *SDB*

Today's Prayer

Father God, thank You for the seeds of encouragement, instruction, and guidance You planted into Your Word long before we even knew we needed them. Help me to call upon the pertinent ones today just at the perfect time. In Jesus' holy name I pray, amen.

Quiet on the Set!

As cold waters to a thirsty soul, so is good news from a far country.

PROVERBS 25:25 KJV

Hollywood never disappoints, does it? No wonder we're inundated with nicknames for the city, like "La-La Land" and "Tinseltown"! Those who live and work near that big white sign on the hill provide us with hours of mystifying entertainment.

And how about DC? Most of us view politicians as wannabe actors in a race to see who's made the morning news. Not a day goes by that some elected official doesn't open his door to accept a subpoena for not paying his taxes, for embezzling money from his campaign fund, for cheating on his spouse. Sometimes there's a news crew on his porch, waiting like hungry hyenas to catch his shocked reaction.

But the media could save its time, because stuff like that is so routine and ordinary that it doesn't even shock me anymore. Is it any wonder Americans are thirsty for *good* news?

I praise Him for blessing me with a loving family, devoted friends, helpful neighbors, and wonderful coworkers, because when the headlines deliver bad tidings, I need only look to them and their everyday achievements for my good news "fix." I'm surrounded by loved ones whose simple, godly lives are a constant source of peaceful inspiration. And if this quiet life ever grows boring, we can count on actors and politicians to spice it up...without ever having to leave the house! ✳ *LL*

Today's Prayer

Thank You, Lord, not only for the many blessings in my life, but for your constant care and love. May I never take them for granted. Amen.

Do You Want Fries with That?

For after all these things the Gentiles seek.
For your heavenly Father knows that you need all these things.
But seek first the kingdom of God and His righteousness,
and all these things shall be added to you.

MATTHEW 6:32–33 NKJV

Honey, while you're up, would you mind getting me a glass of water?"

I glared at my husband and wondered why he always waited until I got up to suddenly want something. I begrudgingly headed to the cupboard, pulled out a glass, then trudged over to the refrigerator to get him some ice water. I'd already forgotten why I got up in the first place.

As I handed my husband his glass of ice water, he took it while his focus never once left the TV screen. Just as I was about to offer up a sarcastic comment, one of my daughters popped in. "Mom, I need a new cell phone. This one doesn't have a camera."

Now I couldn't resist. With sarcasm dripping from my voice, I asked, "Do you want fries with that?"

Suddenly I had my husband's attention. "Huh?"

I smirked at my husband, who sat there and stared at me, his jaw slack and his eyes wide. He clearly thought I'd lost my mind.

"That's just an expression," I explained.

"Oh." He looked at me with concern. "Are you okay?"

Another cutting comment hovered on the tip of my tongue, but I bit it back. With a sigh, I flopped down on the sofa. "I don't know. No matter how much we do, it's never enough." I folded my arms and snorted. "And I feel like a servant around here."

"What's wrong with being a servant?"

I couldn't think of a kind response to that, so I just shrugged.

"Do you think I ask too much of you?" he asked gently.

With a lump in my throat, I slowly nodded. "Yes, sometimes."

I watched as his chin jutted, a look of fierce determination washing over his face. "Girls, you need to come in here. Now."

"But, Daddy..."

"Now," he repeated. "We need to have a family prayer."

One of my girls moaned. "We just prayed at dinner."

Rather than argue, he reached out and took my daughter's hand. As soon as the other one joined us, we bowed our heads and prayed that the Lord would give us all a servant attitude. When we opened our eyes, he looked at me and grinned. "Now is there anything I can do for you?"

✳ DM

Today's Prayer

Dear Lord, You've promised to provide for our needs,
and for that we thank You. Give us the ability to serve each other
with a Christian attitude. Amen.

The Influential Woman

So Esther answered, "If it pleases the king, let the king and Haman
come today to the banquet that I have prepared for him."
...So the king and Haman went to the banquet....
The king said to Esther, "What is your petition? It shall be granted you.
What is your request, up to half the kingdom? It shall be done!"

ESTHER 5:4–6 NKJV

*B*elieve it or not, women have a lot of power in their homes. My
sons used to laugh and jokingly say, "If Mama ain't happy,
nobody's happy." This phrase was usually thrown around on cleaning day
when my poor sons were tortured into picking up their bedrooms (I say
that facetiously). However, there's some truth to the cliché. The Bible
says, "The wise woman builds her house, but the foolish pulls it down
with her hands" (Proverbs 14:1 NKJV).

Amazingly, we women have some mysterious ability to destroy
our husbands, sons, and daughters with abusive words and thoughtless
actions. We have some inexplicable influence over our husbands, too,
like Queen Esther, who saved the entire Jewish nation by persuading her
husband to defeat the man seeking Israel's destruction. Yeah, I guess you
could say she "buttered up" the king with the banquet before springing
her request on him. But you know what they say: Attitude is everything.
Esther had to make sure that God prepared the king's heart, and we all
know that the way to a man's heart is through his stomach.

Seriously, I think today's biblical passage goes to show that if we
wives approach our husbands correctly, we can have a mighty hand in
effectively running our homes. I don't mean to diminish a single mom's
power in the home, but let's face it: It tends to be more difficult to work
ideas around a hardheaded man who happens to live under the same
roof. And if we're stubborn, determined, and overly ambitious, we can

influence our husbands into making unwise decisions. Consequently, we may suffer for it. I think many times women have that much power in their homes, but they just don't realize it.

I also believe there's real-live spiritual warfare going on, and Satan knows that if he is able to destroy a marriage, the institution of family, he can destroy a nation. But a godly woman, like the stuff Queen Esther was made of, can build up or restore her home and her family through faith and prayer. ✳ AKB

Today's Prayer

Father God, help us be Queen Esthers in our homes.
Help us love and respect our husbands. Fill our homes
with the kind of peace, joy, and harmony that only
comes from knowing You. We'll give You the glory for it, Lord Jesus.
In Your name we ask, amen.

The Character of True Love

Love suffers long and is kind; love does not envy;
love does not parade itself, is not puffed up;
does not behave rudely, does not seek its own,
is not provoked, thinks no evil;
does not rejoice in iniquity, but rejoices in the truth;
bears all things, believes all things, hopes all things, endures all things.
Love never fails.

1 CORINTHIANS 13:4–8 NKJV

Karen and I became best friends very soon after our first meeting. We made each other laugh, even in the awful times, and we trusted each other with our deepest concerns and fears. We were prayer partners, girlfriends, sisters.

When I was diagnosed with uterine cancer, Karen was the first person I turned to. She confessed right away that she wasn't sure she could face the battle ahead, but despite this fact, I had faith in the strength I'd always drawn from her friendship, and I reminded her that this was what we were given to battle. I was confident that we could face it together.

One of the things that often occurs with cancer patients between diagnosis and treatment is that their filters shut down. The way they talk to their family and friends, the way they behave in general, is colored by the anger and fear and roller-coaster emotions that they haven't had the time or ability to process. I was terrified, and I just couldn't get a handle on how to face what was littering the road ahead of me. This is no excuse for harsh words or touchy reactions; it's just an explanation.

To say that I was less than soft-spoken and kind would be a gross understatement, and Karen took the brunt of it in those first days.

Still, I've never been more shocked than when I received a curt two-line e-mail from her saying that I should find someone else to take me to the hospital for my surgery; she wouldn't be picking me up. I called her, I e-mailed her, I reached out to her in every way I could think of, believing that an apology was warranted and, afterward, there would be forgiveness and understanding. And restoration.

Almost five years have passed since that e-mail from Karen. Despite my best efforts, I've never heard another word from her. She never knew that the first surgery for the uterine cancer revealed Stage 3 ovarian cancer, as well. She never knew how I struggled through two more surgeries and five weeks of daily radiation, or how alone I felt without her. For nearly three years afterward, I fought bitterness and disappointment, anger and the intense pain that comes with that sort of abandonment. It took three solid years before I could think of her without crying or begin the walk down the road toward forgiving her.

I am happy to report that, with the ability to forgive Karen at last, the Lord has also brought me this revelation knowledge: Forgiving Karen is a blessing to *my heart*, not hers; and people are going to fail you every day of the week, but true love, which is the very character of God Himself, never will. ✳ *SDB*

Today's Prayer

Thank You, Lord, for teaching me about love through Your Word and Your grace. Help me today to remember that, though people will probably let me down in myriad profound ways, love never will. Help me to love them in spite of their failings, with a true and pure heart that shows them Your heart beating through me. In Jesus' precious name I pray, amen.

A Thorny Situation

I am the rose of Sharon,
and the lily of the valleys.
SONG OF SOLOMON 2:1 KJV

It was a small prayer, one that some might call insignificant. "Don't waste God's precious time on a plea that your silly roses will flourish!" said one of my husband's relatives.

But I asked anyway.

Why?

Because I'm convinced it's the very reason I gather more than beautiful blooms from the thorny bushes and why I'm able to take such joy in every velvety petal!

When powdery mildew threatened to overtake the plantings in my garden, I performed every trick in the "How to Grow Roses" handbook.

Once I got that situation under control, aphids invaded—but stubborn determination (and a book called *Roses for Dummies*) solved that problem, too.

Summer's drought continued. Then spider mites set up housekeeping among the prickly stalks. My poor flowers budded but they didn't have the strength to bloom. And, oh, how I missed the delectable scent of my ruby red Mr. Lincolns!

Still I refused to cry "uncle"! On my knees, pruning the brown-spotted yellow lower leaves of my White Ladies, I prayed that the Lord would tell me what to do to save these, His oh-so-lovely creations. And no sooner had I uttered "Amen" than a ladybug zoomed in and then settled on a snowy bud. Soon I realized that she'd brought a couple hundred of her closest friends and relatives along for the flight, for I began noticing black-dotted red beetles on the blooms and leaves of every plant...and dozens more marching toward the hearts of my prized roses.

But it was as a praying mantis clung to one spiky stalk that I knew God didn't consider my prayer insignificant at all, for He'd sent a mini army of six-legged soldiers to protect His delightful roses.

How humbled I was, how blessed I felt, knowing that He *wants* to attends to our every need and desire—even those that others see as a waste of His time! ✳ ℒℒ

Today's Prayer

O heavenly Father of all living things, thank You for the blessings
I find in Your roses. Your glory shines forth in these frilly,
fancy plants and glows just as brightly in the more ordinary marigold
and zinnia that bloom alongside them. Just as You continue
blessing me with a bounty of beauty that grows beneath my windows,
bless me, too, with a heart that is grateful for every bright light
these small flowers bring into the world! Amen.

My Way

Now a leper came to Him, imploring Him,
kneeling down to Him and saying to Him,
"If You are willing, You can make me clean."
Then Jesus, moved with compassion,
stretched out His hand and touched him,
and said to him, "I am willing; be cleansed."
As soon as He had spoken, immediately the leprosy left him,
and he was cleansed.

MARK 1:40–42 NKJV

Between working hard all my life at various jobs and being the best wife and mother I can be, I feel like it's time to have things my way. What's wrong with that? Isn't getting what we deserve the ultimate goal?

Fortunately for all of us, it's not.

Stay with me on this. Yeah, I've been a good wife and mother. My husband is happy and well-fed. My children have grown up to be productive Christian adults. As an employee, I showed up on time, completed all my tasks in the best way I knew how, and showed loyalty toward whatever company I worked for.

So why shouldn't I get what I deserve?

Well, for starters, I'm not Jesus. He's the only perfect person who ever walked the earth. Behind my "good woman" facade is a dirty rotten sinner. I don't set out to do bad things, but terrible thoughts creep into my head. Sometimes what I want is more important to me than the needs of others. I get angry, and I feel left out. When someone who doesn't seem as deserving as me gets something I want, I harbor harsh feelings. I get sick and tired of stuff that is insignificant in the big scheme of things.

In other words, I lose sight of my purpose in this life, which is to glorify Jesus.

This attitude should be in everything I do—from how I talk to people to the way I pray to God. Do I ask for a list of things I think I deserve? Or do I lay my heart on the line and ask that His will be done?

Even though I think I know what's good for me, the only One who truly knows is God. When we pray, we need to remember that what we want is often shiny on the outside but dirty on the inside. Our way isn't necessarily His way. The Lord's will is all-knowing and all good. Like a parent who forces a child to eat her vegetables, He knows what will make us strong in our walk with Him. ✳ DM

Today's Prayer

As I bring my prayers to You, Lord, keep me mindful of Your will.
Give me the knowledge and the power to be ever faithful to You,
even when I don't get what I ask for. Only You know what I truly need. Amen.

Only Believe

"The LORD your God in your midst, the Mighty One, will save;
He will rejoice over you with gladness,
He will quiet you with His love,
He will rejoice over you with singing."

ZEPHANIAH 3:17 NKJV

It's totally amazing to me that our almighty God, the One who created the heavens and the earth, the moon and the stars, is always nearby—there whenever I need Him. When I'm afraid or anxious, He calms me down. He loves me, and He's actually jazzed that I'm part of His family.

What about you?

I realize this biblical truth is hard to fathom if you're a person who has emerged from a less than perfect past. To think that a heavenly Father would "rejoice over you" with gladness and singing doesn't quite compute when an earthly dad has been abusive. The simple act of believing is often complicated by negative outside influences.

In her best-selling book entitled *Battlefield of the Mind Devotional*, Joyce Meyer wrote: "You may have had a miserable past; you may even be in current circumstances that are very negative and depressing. You may be facing situations that are so bad it seems you have no real reason to hope. But I say to you boldly: Your future is not determined by your past or your present!" She goes on to urge readers to "start believing God's Word is true."

I made that very decision to believe God years ago. I had come from a Wednesday night church service in which I heard the gospel. I felt confused about what the Bible teaches regarding salvation, but then, as I stood in front of my kitchen sink washing dishes, I realized my need for God. I prayed, feeling like I wasn't worthy of such a gift, and asked Jesus

Christ into my life, my heart. Then and there I felt a peace flow over me and I knew my prayer had been heard—and answered. I knew biblical truth was the right and only truth. I believed God. After that day an entire universe of hope and blessing opened up to me.

It can happen for you, too! Only believe. ✳ *AKB*

Today's Prayer

Dearest heavenly Father, Your love for us is so amazing.
We might think we're unlovable or unforgivable, but Your Word
says something different. Today we promise to take steps toward believing
that what You say is true. We accept the love You offer us and rest in
Your peace. We thank You for it. In Jesus' name, amen.

Battlefield of the Mind Devotional by Joyce Meyer was published by Warner Faith in 2005.

Bossy Bosserson

Confess your trespasses to one another,
and pray for one another, that you may be healed.
The effective, fervent prayer of a righteous man avails much.

JAMES 5:16 NKJV

Carole had been a project manager for something like ten years, so most of the editors in my department had worked with her at one time or another. I had what I considered to be the misfortune of being assigned to a half dozen different projects with Carole at the helm.

She was often the butt of private jokes about the "criminally organized," and team members would sometimes salute her as she passed. She'd gained the nickname of Bossy Bosserson, but it was only used quietly in certain circles.

One afternoon following an extremely long conference call, I went downstairs to the cafe for a cappuccino—and I noticed Carole sitting alone in the corner, nursing a cup of tea. After I grabbed my coffee and headed for the door, I glanced back at her and saw that she was crying.

Every instinct I had told me to keep on going, but for some reason I just couldn't do it. I approached her cautiously and then slipped into the chair across from her.

"Carole, is there something I can do for you? Can I get you some more tea?"

At first, she glared at me. And then her face just seemed to melt like hot wax, into the saddest grimace I'd ever seen, and tears cascaded down her face in streams.

"I'm sorry. Please just leave me alone," she said.

I finally agreed, and I left her there despite my reluctance to do so.

That day, I started praying for Carole. Every now and then at first, but then each time she came to mind. I prayed for her broken heart and for her tendency to steamroll over her coworkers. I asked the Lord to touch her in some way, in whatever way she needed so badly, and to reveal Himself to her.

"Oh, Lord, just help her to be...nice. She's so miserable that she makes everyone around her miserable, too. Bossy needs a huge dose of Your kindness."

Less than a month later, I found myself sitting in that same spot where I'd seen Carole sipping her tea. This time she took the chair across from me, and she smiled.

"You're far away," she observed.

"I'm just thinking about our meeting this afternoon."

"Well, I want you to know that I think you're doing a wonderful job," she said. "I don't think I tell you that often enough."

I've seldom come face-to-face with such profound answered prayer, but to this day, Bossy Bosserson is a living memorial to me, proving that fervent prayer does indeed avail much. ✳ *SDB*

Today's Prayer

Lord Jesus, thank You for teaching us how to pray. Remind me today and every day that our prayers for others are part of our walk on this earth. Seeing them answered is the fuel that keeps us petitioning for Your hand on our lives. In Your holy name I pray, amen.

Oh Happy Day

Do not be anxious about anything,
but in everything, by prayer and petition,
with thanksgiving, present your requests to God.

PHILIPPIANS 4:6–7 NIV

At the start of every year, I unwrap my new calendar and immediately flip to the August page. And though the weather outside my window is bitterly cold and blustery winds send the snow into drifts, I pray for warmth as the thermometer refuses to budge above zero and ask the Father to allow me a few memories of "heat and humidity" as my gaze locks on a photo of a shorts-and-T-shirts-clad family, who are happily picnicking under an azure sky. I can almost feel the warmth of the sticky breeze, and I thank God for the momentary respite from winter.

Considering the sweltering heat that's commonplace in August, it's no surprise that the month was named for Augustus Caesar, one of history's most hotheaded rulers. I pity my oldest daughter and little sister, both born in August (and stuck with that sickly peridot birthstone), and I cringe, because the flower of their month is the gladiolus...which is so often favored in funeral bouquets.

On a brighter note, though, Ecuador, Korea, India, Indonesia, and Uruguay are among the countries that won their independence during August. In Scotland, people attend the Edinburgh Festival, while in other European countries, citizens and tourists celebrate "workers' day," all in August. Here in the States, August is Picnic Month, Inventors' Month, Back to School Month, and, believe it or not, Catfish Month.

Presidents Benjamin Harrison, Herbert Hoover, Lyndon Johnson, and Bill Clinton were born in August, while on the other side of "life," historical August newspapers reported that Wild Bill Hickok was shot dead in a

Deadwood saloon, Gertrude Ederle became the first woman to swim the English Channel, and Liz Taylor divorced Richard Burton (for the second time) in August. Elvis died and Hurricane Katrina struck...in August.

My parents, in-laws, and my husband and I share an August anniversary. So as I stare at the cloud-dotted sky and the sea of emerald lawn that flows on the August page of a calendar so new that it still wafts the scent of ink, I'm reminded of the plaque above my desk that reads, GOD LOVES AUGUST! ✳ ℒℒ

Today's Prayer

O heavenly Father, never let us get too busy to remember the little things,
like the tropical heat of August, that You have provided to warm us,
just by thinking about it—all year long! Amen.

I Approve This Message

Your word is a lamp to my feet and a light to my path.
I have sworn and confirmed that I will keep Your righteous judgments.
PSALM 119:105–106 NKJV

How many times in 2008 did we hear the phrase "I approve this message"? In the context of the presidential race, everyone understood that the candidate was simply confirming that he or she had the final say before the commercial was aired. But if we think about the significance of those same words in another situation, they could mean something completely different.

As a product information writer for a major television retailer, my job was to write copy for the Web, for call-center representatives, and for show hosts. Before I wrote the first word, each item had passed through the hands of the buyer, quality assurance, and, if necessary, the legal department. By the time I had the silk blouse or leather handbag in my queue, I was fairly certain that the spec sheets were accurate.

When I hit the final button on my computer to post the description on the Web, I was essentially saying "I approve this message" for everyone at the company. If the customer received the item and discovered that any of my words were untrue, someone could lose his or her job—so I was always extremely careful to check or double-check anything that didn't seem accurate. Occasionally an error would slip through in one of the early stages of the process, and the spec sheets would need to be changed. Anyone in the lineup could question the information, so by the time it hit the air or the Web, it had passed the approval of several people.

In another circumstance, the same statement could have still a different meaning. Think about how children rely on a parent's approval. While one child may have permission to walk to the store

165

alone, another might not. When my children were little, they weren't allowed to watch PG-13 movies unless I'd either prescreened them or I was right there beside them with my finger on the remote control FAST-FORWARD button. One day my older daughter came home and said she was the only kid in the entire world whose mother did this. Although I doubt this was accurate, I suspect that there were quite a few parents who gave their children free rein with movies and TV.

Early in my Christian life, even before the WWJD bracelet rage, I heard someone in my church comment that he made his decisions based on what he thought Jesus would want him to do. That stuck in my head, and I still hear that voice when I'm tempted to stray, no matter how right it feels.

Knowing that God is constantly watching can be disconcerting sometimes—particularly when I look with longing at something I know I shouldn't have, see, hear, or do. And that happens way more often than I would like. However, it also gives me a peaceful spirit, knowing that a moment of giving in to something He doesn't approve of, no matter how wonderful it seems at the moment, isn't anything compared to the heavenly treasures He promises. And even when we fail to please Him, His mercy and grace endure with the ultimate approval of our faith in Jesus. ✻ DM

Today's Prayer

Lord, even when I don't show it, I'm grateful for Your protection, mercy, and grace. I pray that You'll continue to shine Your light through me so others can see that the only approval we ultimately need is Yours. Amen.

Calling All Neglected Moms!

Then He said to the disciple, "Behold your mother!"
And from that hour that disciple took her to his own home.

JOHN 19:27 NKJV

"Why don't you call me?"

"Mom, I'm busy."

"Listen, I'm busy, too, but how long does it take to pick up the phone, dial my number, and say, 'Hi, Mom, hope you're okay. Everything's good with me'? It would take all of thirty seconds."

My hardheaded son refuses to see my point. "I'm working two jobs and going to school."

I reply with an exasperated sigh. *No excuse*, I think to myself. After all, Jesus took time to remember His mother while dying on the cross!

Can you imagine being Mary and watching your son die an agonizing death? What a horror. Of course, Jesus' plan, even while dying on the cross, was to return three days later. Even so, it amazes me that our Lord made provisions for His mother even as He suffered, paying for the sins of all humanity.

But my adult son can't even give me a phone call once a week?

When I tell this to my son, his voice hardens. "Mom, Jesus is God. I'm just a normal person!"

"Oh, fine. I'll quit nagging. Just call me once in a while, okay?"

I hang up the phone and my conscience pricks. Maybe I was too hard on him. Are my expectations really too high? I mean, I'm asking my son for a lousy phone call, not a million bucks!

I fume as I go about my business around the house. After all I did for my sons, they can't even call me. Humph!

Later, my husband tells me that my mother called.

I wave a hand at him. "I'll call her later. I don't really feel like talking at the moment."

But then realization hits: I haven't been the most faithful in calling my mother. I mean, I call when I feel like it. She's always there for me. If she's busy, she calls me back. And she listens to me prattle on, sometimes for an hour or more.

Isn't that what moms are supposed to do? Be there for their kids, whenever they happen to call and want to chitchat? Of course, circumstances may prevent moms from calling or receiving phone calls at the moment, but then the call's returned when there is time. Basic courtesies.

Hmm...

The decision made, I pick up the telephone. "Hi, Mom, I'm just returning your phone call." ✻ AKB

Today's Prayer

Dearest Lord in heaven, it's so easy to demand our rights as parents but to slip in our responsibility as adult children. You tell us to honor our parents—no matter what kind of people they were during our growing-up years—or who they are now. Help us to respect our parents, just as we respect and honor You, our heavenly Father— and just as we want our children to love and respect us.

In Jesus' name, amen.

Dry Your Tears

You number my wanderings;
put my tears into Your bottle...
PSALM 56:8 NKJV

I'm convinced that every woman has that *one guy* in her past: the one who made her cry until she didn't think she had a tear left to shed; the one who fooled her once and then fooled her twice but, despite it all, she leapt over the old adage to open the door and let him in to fool her yet again.

Mark was that guy for me. Our relationship spanned many years, but we never seemed to have more than a month of happiness before another bump in the road threw us off course. By the time that last breakup klunked along, it wasn't a thrill to ride the roller coaster any more; it was just exhausting. I'd learned not to trust in the love I felt for him, because every time I leaned against it for a few minutes, it gave way and I went tumbling.

We'd agreed on a birthday gift for his mother, a beautiful gold locket we'd had engraved. I carefully placed photos of Mark and his sister inside and eagerly sprinted up the sidewalk toward his front door. His mom was going to love it!

My hand was poised and I was ready to give the screen door a couple of raps when I noticed that the front door was cracked open. When I looked inside, I saw Mark on the sofa with another woman in his arms. I stood there like a statue, my hand still raised and ready to knock, my mouth gaping open in a perfect round *O*, and my eyes so wide I couldn't even blink.

It was like a scene out of a really bad movie. He looked up at me over her shoulder and our eyes met, but he didn't say a word. When I finally found my breath, I dropped the velvet box with the locket on the porch and spun around, rushing away from his house. It wasn't until much later that I realized he hadn't even bothered to follow me. The other woman in his embrace didn't even know what had occurred. I looked in my rearview mirror to see if his front door had at least opened. It hadn't. I was heartbroken.

The phone calls started coming two hours later, and they kept coming for three straight days. On the second day came the lavender roses, my favorites, followed that night by the first of a dozen e-mails that I deleted without reading. All the ploys that had been successful in reuniting us in the past just cascaded on my deaf ears and numb heart. I cried on the first night, but after that my tear ducts had at last gone dry.

I prayed and asked the Lord many times in those days why, this time, it felt different, and about a week later I opened my Bible and began to read the first scripture that caught my eye: "You number my wanderings; put my tears into Your bottle...."

So that was it, I realized. Mark had made me cry so often and so violently, so many times. Over those years, the Lord had no doubt saved up my tears, and now I had a credit coming. I e-mailed Mark that night and asked him not to contact me again. I told him I was finished with the roller coaster, and I haven't ridden one since. Literally or figuratively.
✲ *SDB*

Today's Prayer

Thank You, Lord, for keeping such a close eye on me that You keep track of
every hair on my head and keep every one of my tears in Your bottle.
Help me today to remember that, despite the emotions that want to
tell me otherwise, I am not alone. I never was.
In Your precious name I pray, amen.

The Wolf and His Shadow

But they measuring themselves by themselves,
and comparing themselves among themselves, are not wise.

2 CORINTHIANS 10:12 KJV

If you play an audiotape of someone and ask that same person whose voice it is, nine out of ten will say they have no idea. Point out a habit or personality quirk and chances are good you'll be treated to a "Who, *me*?" expression. Why? Simple! We rarely see ourselves the way others do.

If someone asked me to name my biggest flaw, I'd say "Impatience." Asked which character trait is my most positive, I'd answer "Hardworking," "Bighearted," or "Self-sacrificing,"...depending on the mood or circumstance I'm in.

But if I'm truly hardworking, why can't my husband see it and accept as fact that the time I spend updating Facebook is a legitimate promotional effort? If I'm so bighearted, why does my dog look so wounded after I snarl, "You were outside five times in the past hour, so leave me alone"? When I spout a quick and firm "Can't!"—do the people who ask me to bake cupcakes, Hike for a Cure, or donate $75 so inner-city kids can attend the circus really think I'm self-sacrificing?

Unless we're clones of Mother Theresa, we're all guilty of duplicity like that from time to time, and it doesn't make us inherently dishonest. Or mean. Or horrible Christians. All it makes us is *human.*

I'm reminded of Aesop's fable, "The Wolf and His Shadow." As the story goes, the wolf's shadow made him appear a hundred times his actual size, making him feel stronger and braver than he had a right to feel. So when a powerful lion happened along, the wolf believed *he* could become king of the beasts. And as he strutted, still admiring his shadow, the lion flattened him with a single blow. The moral of the story? Do not let self-flattery make you forget who—and what—you truly are.

I'm in as much danger of becoming "lion prey" as any full-blown narcissist—if I allow myself to measure my worth by my own benchmarks. ✳ *LL*

Today's Prayer

My Lord, command me to love myself last. Give me a heart that knows
no greed, no selfishness, no foolish pride. Bless me with a spirit that
recognizes always that You alone have earned others' praises.
Keep me ever mindful that although I stand before You a sinner,
I deserve Your love, because You made the ultimate sacrifice...for me!
Thank You, Jesus, for making me aware of the feelings of others and for
keeping me "small," especially in my own eyes. Never allow my needs
to overshadow those of others. Amen.

Living Life at Warp Speed

My brethren, count it all joy when you fall into various trials,
knowing that the testing of your faith produces patience.
JAMES 1:2–3 NKJV

With life demanding so much of our time these days, we have thirty hours' worth of things to do in a twenty-four-hour day. Who has time to relax and regenerate?

There's nothing like an accident, injury, or sickness to slow us down. On my early morning commute to work about two years ago, I sat at a red light, grinding my teeth about how bad the traffic was and how irritating it was that I'd missed the green light. Suddenly I felt a quick jolt and heard a popping sound. A quick glance at my rearview mirror let me know that the woman who'd been tailgating me for the past mile had miscalculated the distance between us, and she hadn't been able to stop before our cars made contact.

As I got out to check on the damage, I was amazed by the woman's skill at being able to juggle coffee in one hand and her cell phone in the other. And she was still jabbering into the phone, too, saying words I won't repeat! She tossed me a look of annoyance, but until I told her I was calling the police, she didn't flip her phone shut. Finally, she let me know she was late for an appointment and she didn't have time for this. I had to bite my tongue to prevent me from saying what was on my mind. Instead, I took a deep breath, ran my hand over the small nicks her bumper had made in mine, and told her that I was okay if she didn't want to bother with the police since my car seemed all right. She squinted as she studied her own bumper that had a little more damage than mine, before snorting and heading back to her own car. I stood there for a moment, stunned that she didn't have the decency to say another word before she gunned her engine and left. The one other person who'd stopped said he had her license plate number if I needed it in the future. I accepted it, thanked him, and went on to work.

After that incident, I changed my attitude toward the whole daily commute. Rather than fretting over getting to work on time, I gave myself more time by leaving five or ten minutes earlier. The Lord gave us twenty-four-hour days with at least a third of that time meant for sleep. He knows what we need better than we do, so why push for something we can't have? I've always been production-driven, so this is difficult for me, but I'm working on it. ✳ DM

Today's Prayer

Dear heavenly Father, You've provided the time I need for living my life the way You intended. Be with me as I work on living each minute to glorify You rather than force my own timing into everything. Amen.

Is That You, God?

Then He said, "Go out, and stand on the mountain before the Lord."
And behold, the Lord passed by, and a great and strong wind
tore into the mountains and broke the rocks in pieces before the Lord,
but the Lord was not in the wind; and after the wind an earthquake,
but the Lord was not in the earthquake; and after the earthquake a fire,
but the Lord was not in the fire; and after the fire a still small voice.

1 Kings 19:11–12 nkjv

I used to think God looked and sounded like the Great Oz—you know, that round white face in the movie *The Wizard of Oz* who boomed out his replies and made Dorothy quake with fear in her sparkling ruby slippers. But as my relationship with God developed, I realized that my image of Him was far from accurate.

The Bible tells us in Genesis that God made man "in His own image" (Genesis 1:27 nkjv) and that He called for Adam and Eve as He was "walking in the garden in the cool of the day" (Genesis 3:8 nkjv). After studying that verse, I believed God actually walked around, enjoying His creation. Later in that same book, the Bible states, "But the Lord came down to see the city and the tower which the sons of men had built" (Genesis 11:5 nkjv). He actually left heaven to see what was happening on earth! So much for my "white round face" theory. The truth is, God walks and talks and seeks our fellowship. Amazing!

So many people have wacky assumptions about who the person of God is and what He is like. Some picture Him as an angry God, ready to consume anybody who steps out of line. Others see him as an impersonal but powerful spirit. But that's not how the Bible describes God. He feels our pain, shares our frustrations, rejoices in our accomplishments, and cheers when we succeed. He calms our fears, and He has promised to protect us from all that is evil. He has promised to provide for our needs, and I have personally witnessed that fact. I have learned that the God of heaven is my beloved Savior and Friend.

Some months ago my husband and I had no income, as we were both self-employed. Our savings was spent and our checking accounts were empty. We didn't have that month's mortgage payment or the car payments, and the utility bills were due. I remember crying out to God, and I heard His "still small voice" speak to my heart, saying, "Even if you lose it all, I still have a plan for you."

The reply gave me such hope and peace. I didn't have to worry myself sick about our dilemma. It all belonged to God anyway. And I believed from that day forward that the Lord would provide for my husband and me. Suddenly I couldn't wait to see what He would do!

A few weeks later, an unexpected check arrived in the mail. Daniel and I were totally amazed and extremely grateful. The sum covered our mortgage and our bills and there was even some left over!

God is able!

Those three words sound so simple, so trite, and yet they ring so true. All we need to do is open our hearts and hear Him when He speaks to us and then believe.

Shhh...are you listening? ✳ AKB

Today's Prayer

Precious Lord, thank You for being You, an almighty, powerful,
yet sensitive and all-knowing God. You have given us eternal life,
and You love us unconditionally. Help us to hear Your "still small voice,"
even through the din of life. Deepen our relationship with You.
Help us to feel Your presence every hour of every day. In Jesus' name, amen.

Gimme, Gimme

Now it came to pass, as He was praying in a certain place,
when He ceased, that one of His disciples said to Him,
"Lord, teach us to pray, as John also taught his disciples."

LUKE 11:1 NKJV

Gimme one of those cookies!"

My friend's head slowly swiveled until she stared deliberately at her six-year-old son, who stood on the other side of the counter. She seemed to be burning a hole right into him, and little Ethan began to melt around it.

"Ethan David, what did you say to me?"

The boy glanced at me, and a wave of crimson moved over his face and chest. Then he looked almost pitifully at his mother.

"I'm sorry, Mommy. May I have a cookie?"

"You may. Just one." And as he timidly took an oatmeal-raisin cookie from the plate between us, she added, "What do you say?"

"Thank you."

"And?"

"And excuse me."

Alison had taught her son well. He knew better than to barge into the kitchen, interrupt a conversation we were having, and demand a cookie—but Ethan's six-year-old enthusiasm had gotten the better of him. When he was reminded to step back and think about what he'd been taught, however, he was able to produce the desired results as well as please his mother.

We've been taught how to pray. We know that there is a certain etiquette to our prayers, but not a script. The Lord's Prayer guides us through.

First, there is gratitude and reverence for our God (*"hallowed be Thy name*"); then there is submission to His plan for our lives ("*Thy will be done*"); and we confess our sins, knowing that He is just and loving and willing to forgive ("*forgive us our trespasses*"); and so forth.

As in all things in life, there is a method to God's teachings and an inexplicable joy for the spirit when those teachings are engrained upon our hearts. Like Ethan, we may often burst into prayer with our frustrations and earthly desires, but there is a joy in entering first with praise for a loving and forgiving God who wants to hear about our hopes and dreams, even though He already knows every one of them intimately. ✻ *SDB*

Today's Prayer

Lord, You are a magnificent and wonderful God. And You are also
a personal confidant for all of my fears and aspirations.
Thank You for loving me in the omnipotent way that You do,
thank You for Your forgiveness and restoration, and thank You
for teaching me how to draw closer to You every day.
I am a servant of the Most High God. In Jesus' name I pray, amen.

Quiet Time

Therefore, my beloved brethren, be ye steadfast, unmoveable,
always abounding in the work of the Lord....

1 CORINTHIANS 15:58 KJV

The cowboys of the old West were blessed with a wonderful gift for defining ordinary, everyday events in the most exciting and fascinating ways. Take, for example, "blazing star"—their description of a stampede of pack animals. If you ever see one, you'll instantly realize how accurate—and how poetic—their term is, as you watch the herd simultaneously burst in every direction, scattering like stardust.

I'm not proud to declare that I identify with those four-legged critters, because with very little distraction, my brain can blast off to who knows where, leaving whatever I might have been doing undone. At least until the Lord leads me back to my desk and reminds me of the assignment He's given.

Too many well-meaning friends and relatives who fancy themselves armchair shrinks have suggested that I might be afflicted with a touch of Attention Deficit Disorder...and when they spout their proclamation, it pleases me no end to announce, "I've been tested, and the pros say no to that!"

So if my problem isn't ADD, what explains my occasional inability to focus?

To put it simply, I've forgotten to ask God to ground me with steadfastness, forgotten that *He* is immovable, that His *Word* is immovable, and that my faith needs to be immovable, too. "I am the LORD," says Malachi 3:6, "I change not" (KJV). (Y'think maybe if I read that verse enough times, the message will sink in deep enough to keep me on task, all through my days?)

It's doable if I remind myself, often, that the finale of 1 Corinthians

15:58 says, "forasmuch as ye know that your labour is not in vain in the Lord" (KJV).

Should be pretty simple, shouldn't it, when the answer to my question isn't some well-guarded secret but a black-and-white biblical truth: If I busy myself *not* with things of an earthly nature but with *His* work....

Good thing I have Him to lean on, isn't it, when my brain goes off like a blazing star! ✳ ℒℒ

Today's Prayer

O divine Creator, teach me what it means to truly abide in You,
my all-knowing force of life! Bless me with clear-eyed awareness
of my purpose here on earth so I'll never mistake trivial "human duties"
for those tasks You have called me to perform. Give me the good judgment
and farsightedness, Father, to make wise use of every hour You've granted me,
for I truly desire to walk a life of Christian steadfastness. Amen.

I'm the Mom, That's Why

Honor your father and your mother, that your days may be long upon the land which the LORD your God is giving you.

EXODUS 20:12 NKJV

I had one of the most profound experiences of my life in early 2009. My firstborn, Alison, gave birth to my first grandchild. As her husband, Jason, and I stood beside her while she was in labor, I couldn't help but flash back to when she was born. What a life-changing experience!

Now that Alison, Jason, and Emma are home from the hospital, I see the impact that one tiny baby can have on so many. People from all over are flying and driving to see this newly expanded family. Diets have changed to accommodate the needs of a nursing child. The dog and cat have new positions in the family—still important and loved but no longer the primary focus of maternal and paternal energy. The once-minimalist decor has changed to "early baby." Two loving parents are willing to sacrifice sleep, money, and everything else they once valued to ensure the safety and contentment of their precious child.

My favorite aspect of this whole experience is how I can see the fruits of my own sacrifices for my daughter. As she grew and developed, I sometimes wondered if I was doing the best for her. Now that she's a mother, I have no doubt that the best and most important thing my husband and I did was share the love of Christ. Alison and Jason are already discussing spiritual issues for Emma. They want to bring her up among other believers so she'll have every advantage possible in today's insane world.

Being a parent is difficult, even with the best and most well-behaved children. I have no doubt that Alison and Jason are up to the task as long as they keep Christ at the forefront of their lives. As Emma grows and develops, she'll test her parents—because that's what children do. With the guidance of biblical principles, they'll help her understand that the Lord's ways are greater than her own.

As I obnoxiously share photos of my first grandchild with anyone who'll stand still long enough to look, I have to remember that, first, she's a child of God. And every night before I go to sleep, I thank Him for blessing Alison and Jason with such a darling child. ✳ DM

Today's Prayer

Thank You, God, for the blessing of Your precious child Jesus.
May Your sacrifice be acknowledged and honored every single day
in our home. Amen.

I Am Really Ticked Off!

*For the wrath of man does not produce
the righteousness of God.*

JAMES 1:20 NKJV

I truly admire John the Baptist. I love his tenacity. I marvel at the way he pointed to Jesus instead of himself. He could have been proud. A multitude of people thought he was the Messiah. He could have given in to the temptation to proclaim himself a great man if nothing else, but he said he was just "the voice of one crying in the wilderness" (John 1:23).

Many times over the years, I have felt like a "voice of one crying in the wilderness," too, but in a very different way. "Clean your room." "Pick up your clothes." Was anybody listening? Hello–o?

That'd make me so angry. But I can honestly tell you now that my anger back then didn't change one single thing.

Even now that my sons are adults I feel like they don't hear me sometimes, and on occasion I feel insulted, angry.

"Listen, I'm important!" I feel like shouting. "I was the one who potty-trained you! Remember *that* the next time you use the men's room!"

Sheesh, the nerve of these kids!

It's at these tumultuous times in my life that God's still, small voice whispers, "Your anger doesn't produce My righteousness."

That's when reality sets in. You see, instead of getting angry, all I need to do is turn to God.

Pastor Joel Osteen, a prominent author and speaker, stated in one of his televised messages that when we get angry, we "give our power away." Anger taps us emotionally. Anger makes our stomachs hurt and gives us headaches. What's more, anger doesn't usually produce the change we desire, although things might change for the worst because of a temper fit. Friends and loved ones might not want to be around us if we're always ticked off about some situation or a negative response we've received along the way.

I guess I've learned that lesson the hard way.

But when we take our anger to the Lord, He can handle it. He's God. He's the One who is able to move mountains and part seas. He can heal the sick—and He can take away our anger and replace it with His perfect peace.

In her book *Praying God's Word Day by Day*, Beth Moore incorporates Matthew 5:34–35 when she writes, "Heaven is Your throne; earth is Your footstool. Therefore, anything over my head is under Your feet."

That includes those situations that really work our last nerve!

✳ *AKB*

Today's Prayer

Dear Lord, there is nothing too big for You to tackle. You are God, and You have promised to be with us and share Your power so that we can handle anything that comes our way. Remind us not to waste our time and energy by being angry and frustrated by small circumstances. Rather, let us use the power You've given us for great and glorious accomplishments. In Jesus' name, amen.

Praying God's Word Day by Day by Beth Moore was published by B&H Books in 2006.

Weary to the Bone

*"Come to Me, all you who labor
and are heavy laden, and I will give you rest."*
Matthew 11:28 nkjv

$\mathcal{Y}$ou're just too Christian for us."

"Wow," I replied dryly. "I didn't know there was such a thing. And is it even legal for you to say that to me?"

It felt like everything I did as an editorial supervisor for two straight years had been scrutinized, judged, or corrected on a personal level. And now having a scripture taped on my computer screen to encourage myself as I fought through a health problem had been reported to the main office as inappropriate. It was just about all I could take.

I left that meeting feeling more tired than I ever knew a person could feel. Weary to the bone and beyond; weary all the way to my soul. I packed up a box of my personal things, offered my resignation, and numbly meandered to the parking lot. My limits had been met and crossed months prior, and I'd been hanging on and enduring for as long as I possibly could. I was finally finished.

When I got home, I dropped the cardboard box with my coffee mug and framed photos and sat down in front of the computer. I went directly to a job site and submitted my resume to the first available editorial job I could find. Once I hit the Send button, I started to cry.

Deep within me, I felt the sweet and gentle whisper of my Father: *"Bring me your burdens. I will give you rest."*

I got up from the computer, went into my bedroom, and stretched out facedown across the bed. I cried before the Lord for a solid hour, recounting what He already knew about the challenges and obstacles and strength-zapping battles I'd been waging at my job.

When I'd dried my last tear, I took a deep breath and fell into a fast, hard sleep. It was already dark outside when the ringing of the phone awakened me, and I answered without looking at the caller identification (which I almost never do).

It was the hiring supervisor for the company to which I had applied a few hours earlier. "Your resume is very impressive," she said. "You seem like a perfect fit for the editorial position we've been trying to fill."

That call was the catalyst for one of the best and most fulfilling jobs I've ever had, and it's so comforting to know that the net had been cast beneath me long before I even knew I would need it. While I was still struggling against the current of a job that was taxing everything I had inside me, the Lord had prepared the ground to bless me when the time came to move on. ✳ *SDB*

Today's Prayer

Lord Jesus, I love You for so many things. But in particular, I love You for those times when You catch me in a net that was cast before I even stumbled and fell. Thank You for easing my burdens and for teaching me to lay my fears and challenges at Your feet, where I will surely find rest.

In Your holy name I pray, amen.

What's Your Hurry?

Wait on the LORD; be of good courage,
and he shall strengthen thine heart:
wait, I say, on the LORD.

PSALM 27:14 KJV

*D*id you ever wonder how Oklahomans earned the nickname "Sooners"? Some historians believe that the term's origin dates back to the days when settlers "jumped the gun" and claimed land in the Cherokee Strip before it was legal to do so.

And in the days of the open range, it was common practice for cattlemen to schedule specific dates for the roundups in each area. Rustlers and hustlers who "worked the cows" to get mavericks and slicks (unbranded cows) for themselves—ahead of the roundup—were branded "sooners" by honest cowboys.

It's no surprise, then, to learn that such "haste makes waste" behaviors have roots in the pages of the Good Book. "He that believeth shall not make haste," says Isaiah 28:16. Job's plea in chapter 30, verse 13 was, "They break up my road; they succeed in destroying me—without anyone's helping them" (NIV). John describes how Jewish leaders didn't much like watching victims suffer on the Sabbath, so they asked Pilate to break their legs to hasten their deaths.

So it appears that being in a perpetual hurry hasn't been good for man since, well, the dawn of mankind!

I'm guilty of "making haste" and "hurrying," and though I try to convince others—and myself—that every rush-rush activity is for a very good reason, the fact is, most things simply aren't all that urgent, no matter how convincing my explanations are to the contrary!

What I'm working on in my Quest for a Better Loree is to balance my good intentions and great plans for improving charitable programs, my preferred fund-raising organizations, my own work, and the place I call home alongside my relationship with Christ. I need to heed the safety lessons I stalwartly taught my children: Stop, look, and listen, then ask myself if the good deeds I'm doing are to bring glory to myself... or to my Lord and Savior.

I want to follow where He leads, but how can I know *where* He wants me to go if my brain's all atwitter with to-do list instructions and I'm exhausted from trying to cram three days of work into one twenty-four-hour period?

When I'm stressed out, tired, and feeling "put upon," it's almost always because I've forgotten the wisdom found in Psalm 27:14: "Wait, I say, on the LORD" (KJV).

And if I'm smart, I'll do it "sooner" rather than later! ✳ *LL*

Today's Prayer

Jesus, Lord of All, never take Your eyes from me, for without Your steadfast guidance, this weak-though-well-intended servant might stray too far from Your light! Hold me close and whisper constantly into my ear, "Wait...." Bless me with an ability to discern the difference between what You truly call me to do...and what I think You want from me. Let my greatest desires be the echoes of Your plan for my life. Amen.

Try It—You'll Like It

For in that He Himself has suffered, being tempted,
He is able to aid those who are tempted.
HEBREWS 2:18 NKJV

"If it feels good, why not do it? Who's it going to hurt?"

The temptations of today are greater than ever! As if we didn't have enough desires on our own, TV and radio commercials flaunt one product after another, with the false claim that we "deserve" it all.

Ha! What I think I deserve is some quiet time, away from false desire that will only break me down and distance me from the God I love—the God who saved me through Christ.

Some temptations are more powerful than others. Mine are too much chocolate, too much bread, too much sushi, and too much queso dip with my chips. Put a plate of any of those in front of me, regardless of how much is on that plate, and chances are it'll be gone before I even realize it was there. Of course, this results in extra weight around the waist and hips.

One of my friends was married to a philanderer whose temptation of having extramarital relationships destroyed his marriage, a much more difficult problem to overcome. A lot of people suffered—my friend, her ex-husband, and their children. He tried it and liked it. Her life was turned upside down because of it.

Some people use drugs to feel better. Why not? After all, if it's not hurting anyone else and it makes you feel good, what's the problem? Right?

Well, for one thing, unless it's prescribed by a physician to make you healthier, it's wrong.

Another temptation I've personally witnessed is gossip at the office. Who doesn't want to listen in on a conversation with juicy tidbits about a coworker or the boss? It's easy to justify, too, because it's "work-related." What would happen if at least one person in each group took the high road and spoke up whenever someone had something derogatory to say about another person? The likely scenario is that those who want to gossip will take their "trash talk" somewhere else.

This will put those who choose not to participate at a disadvantage, right?

Not really. If we resist the temptation to do what we know is wrong—whether it's overeat, have an extramarital affair, do something illegal and unethical, or participate in gossip in any way—the Lord will honor our desire to be right with Him. ✳ *DM*

Today's Prayer

Lord, help me stay strong against the temptations constantly threatening to pull me away from You. Give me the strength to say no when something isn't right for me. Guide me toward what is good and right as Your faithful follower. Amen.

Freedom for the Soul

If we confess our sins, He is faithful and just
to forgive us our sins and to cleanse us from all unrighteousness.

1 JOHN 1:9 NKJV

Years ago, I felt justified in calling out a sister in Christ. I told her off; she'd deserved it—or so I thought. Later, to my horror, that woman's husband and another man from church came over to set me straight. The woman's husband was a deacon, and she'd informed him of what had transpired between us. He brought another deacon with him.

Sitting in my living room, the two men were actually very kind in their reprimand. It wasn't long before I realized they were right: I'd let my temper get the best of me. While I didn't use bad language or raise my voice, the way I handled the situation, and my reaction, was wrong.

Faced with the truth, I was humbled. I felt awful. I apologized to my sister-in-Christ, who was said she was sorry, too. Then I begged God's forgiveness. In fact, I repented every fifteen minutes for the next two days. I decided I was a terrible person, a horrible Christian. You see, no one beats me up like *I* beat me up!

My oldest son, who'd been studying for the ministry, noticed I was sad and discouraged. I guess what gave it away was that I'd crawled into bed with the covers pulled up to my chin—at four o'clock in the afternoon.

"I thought that situation was over and done with, Mom," Ben said, leaning against the door frame.

"Not for me. I can't believe I let that happen. Why did I react so badly?"

Ben disappeared for a few minutes then returned with his Bible. "Mom, Proverbs 24:16 says that a righteous man can fall seven times and still get up again. By 'men' God means *mankind*. It means women, too."

"Thanks for the clarification," I quipped. I sat up and pulled the Bible onto my lap. I read the verse.

"Everybody makes mistakes. You tripped, Mom. You fell. But now you have to pick yourself up again." Reaching over, he flipped through the delicate pages of God's Word and found another verse. "Look at this one. It says that if we confess our sins, God is faithful and just to forgive us and cleanse us from all unrighteousness. Did you ask God's forgiveness?"

"Yes. Numerous times."

"Once is enough." He paused. "Don't you believe God?"

"Well, yes, but..." I drew in a deep breath. "Oh, you're right. I'm my own worst enemy."

I slunked out of bed. It occurred to me that if God was faithful and just to forgive me, then I should forgive myself. I needed to pick myself up and go on with my life. To learn from the mistake but not wallow in the guilt.

Years later, the tendency is still there to wallow in guilt whenever I stumble, trip, or fall—like we all do. We all will. We're human and imperfect. But I've learned that forgiveness is key to bypassing guilt and moving forward with life. Forgiveness is, in a word, freeing. ✳ *AKB*

Today's Prayer

Precious Lord, we thank You for Your graciousness. Help us to understand that You are ready and willing to forgive us whenever we come to You and ask. Your Word is true, Father God, and You cannot lie. Help us to believe we are forgiven, even when we might not feel like it at first. In Christ's name, amen.

No Good Deed Goes Unpunished

"Thus says the LORD to you: 'Do not be afraid
nor dismayed because of this great multitude,
for the battle is not yours, but God's.'"

2 CHRONICLES 20:15 NKJV

The public defender assigned to my case laughed at his own wit after telling me, "No good deed goes unpunished in this world." I didn't find it amusing at all.

I'd worked hard to put together a silent auction to raise funds for a children's charity; but when the charity wanted to take over the running of the auction, I first talked it over with my celebrity client who'd been sponsoring the event. We both agreed that, since it was his name and reputation overseeing the details, we wanted to keep it under our wing. He instructed me to collect the auction items we'd been storing in their offices but to assure them that the funds raised would still be turned over to them when all was said and done. We'd done it a dozen times before, and that seemed like the sensible response.

A few hours later, however, the police arrived at my door, and I was faced with the accusation of Grand Theft.

For a Goody Two-Shoes like myself, a brush with law enforcement was a staggering first. Over the course of several weeks, the drama seemed to escalate daily...all because of what had originated as a simple act of kindness on the part of myself and my client.

As I wrestled with what to say to a judge and how best to keep the story concise and factual, I began sleeping less and worrying more. My imagination got the better of me, and the worst *Law and Order* scenarios played out in my mind—most of them ending with me cowering behind bars, holding a tin cup, and wondering how my life had turned out that way. I tried to remind myself that this was not the plan God had for me, that I'd done nothing wrong, and that the outcome would surely be to my benefit.

On the morning of the hearing, I clung to a strip of wrinkled paper shoved deep into my pocket, a note that a friend had sent to remind me that the battle was not mine.

"That battle belongs to God," she wrote. "You're protected and loved."

However, when the hearing started off with a statement being read from my client where he relinquished any responsibility for the ordeal and claimed that I had acted on my own, all my comfort dried up and withered away, and that piece of paper in my pocket offered no further reassurances. I was terrified. And so hurt.

The hearing lasted an excruciating fifty minutes (but it seemed like the whole day), at the end of which all charges against me were dropped. I limped out of the courtroom that day, wrung out and exhausted. It didn't have to be that way, of course, because my friend's note said it all.

That battle waged against me had little, if anything, to do with me. It was about pride and suspicion and mistrust—and probably greed. It was about all the things the Lord has been battling on our behalf since the dawn of time. In truth, that battle belonged to God the whole time, like most of the big ones do.

The little ones, too, come to think of it. ✷ *SDB*

Today's Prayer

Thank You, Jesus, for being my warrior, my champion, and my protector. Help me today to keep the reminder of those roles You play at the forefront of my mind and heart. When the fog thickens and the battlefield appears to shift, help me to remember that the war belongs to You, just as it always has. In the name of Jesus I pray, amen.

Black (Friday) Fat Pants

Take heed to yourselves,
lest at any time your hearts be overcharged
with surfeiting, and drunkenness....

LUKE 21:34 KJV

*D*epartment and discount stores call the day after Thanksgiving "Black Friday" in the hope that their cash drawers will overflow. That's what I call it, too...because it's the day I draw the drapes, bolt the doors, take the phone off the hook, and run around the house in a black leotard, working off the turkey, stuffing, mashed potatoes and gravy, and pumpkin pie and whipped cream I've recently devoured.

I'm big on holiday dinners. And I'm more than happy to carve time from my hectic schedule to prepare meals so large I'm forced to add every leaf to the dining table *and* a card table at each end to make room for centerpieces, main courses, side dishes, assorted breads, and the good china.

I have to snicker, saying that, because the only "good" thing about my china was the $69.95 I plunked down for twelve 5-piece place settings of faux Blue Willow. Ditto the Bohemian crystal water goblets and Paul Revere–styled flatware. If somebody chips one of those cups or loses a fork in the trash as we scrape plates...? No big deal!

I've been told that my "Don't worry about it!" attitude is why not one of the dozens gathered 'round the Lough table complains about squeezing in, shoulder-to-shoulder, between old codgers and damp toddlers, good friends and total strangers. But I don't suppose it hurts that every bowl and platter overflows with tried-and-true recipes...and a few Weight Watchers concoctions, snuck onto the table for good (waist) measure....

I'm no scholar, but I've learned how to make folks believe *mi casa es su casa*. I'm not related to Amy Vanderbilt or Emily Post, but I'll treat you like royalty. And while I'm far from wealthy, I pray you'll leave here richer than when you arrived...in good times and laughter, memories and friendship...and bloated bellies!

Did we need that cornucopia of appetizers and desserts, or Nonna's linen tablecloth and napkins on the table? Were scented candles on the mantel and a glowing fire in the woodstove necessary? Nah, but even those finger-pointin' mamas who taught us to avoid overindulgence look the other way on holidays at my house, as they sneak a second helping of ham or a third slice of homemade pie.

Makes you wonder, doesn't it, how many of *them* wriggle into "fat pants" on Black Friday so they'll be more comfortable on the treadmill or the Exercycle while working off that bowl of Jell-O piled high with whipped cream.

Um...pass the cheesecake, will ya? ✳ *LL*

Today's Prayer

Father, I'm in constant awe of Your ability to lead the lonely
and alone to holiday tables across the globe. I'm so blessed
to witness Your steadfast love as it brings about healing among
feuding family members and turns strangers into friends!
It is my honor, Lord, and my privilege to prepare the food
You so generously provide and serve it with humble gratitude,
for You are my Lord and Savior. Amen.

Fear of Falling

If I say, "My foot slips," Your mercy, O LORD, will hold me up.
In the multitude of my anxieties within me, Your comforts delight my soul.

PSALM 94:18–19 NKJV

I've never been fond of heights. When I look down from what I consider an unnatural height, I get a swirling, light-headed sensation that keeps me far away from the edge of balconies and cliffs. I enjoy going to big cities, but I have to force myself to think happy thoughts as my hotel elevator lifts me to a double-digit floor and deposits me far enough up in the building that if I fell out a window, I'd be in a world of hurt.

I'm one of those people who has falling dreams that startle me awake. Then I have a hard time going back to sleep for fear of a recurring dream.

From a very early age, most people have some degree of a fear of falling. Some psychologists believe that babies respond well to swaddling because it gives them a sense that they're secure and safe from being dropped.

Next time you take your kids to the park, watch them cross the monkey bars. Most of them hold on very tight, and those who have the biggest fears want their parents nearby to catch them in case they fall. Yes, there are exceptions; some children don't seem to mind falling on their heads. They just hop back up on those bars like nothing ever happened. But they're in the minority.

As people grow older, they show this fear in other ways—like by holding onto rails and banisters when climbing stairs. Of course, there are some people who defy that fear, while others watch them in awe as they skydive, bungee jump, or do any other death-defying act that involves falling.

This fear is logical because we instinctively know that if we fall, we're likely to get hurt. Even the expression *falling in love* implies that we lose control, and it can be quite painful.

In Psalm 94:18–19, the Lord promises to hold you up if you slip. This gives me comfort to know that He is there and that I can let go of my anxieties and be assured that I'm well taken care of. I can lean on Him for comfort and not fear falling into evil, as long as I'm being swaddled by His Word. ✳ DM

Today's Prayer

Lord, release me from my fear of falling into evil.
Keep me constantly aware that You are always there
to hold me up and comfort me. In Jesus name, amen.

The World
on a Silver Platter

*"I am the Alpha and the Omega,
the First and the Last."*

REVELATION 1:11 NKJV

There are a lot of people who will attest to the adage that "money isn't everything." It's true. None of us can buy love or happiness or eternal salvation. Only God can meet those innermost needs.

One evening at church we sang an old hymn that reminded me of this very truth.

*Take the world, but give me Jesus—
All its joys are but a name;
But His love abideth ever,
Thru eternal years the same.*

*O the height and depth of mercy!
O the length and breadth of love!
O the fullness of redemption—
Pledge of endless life above.*
Fanny J. Crosby (1820–1915)

We live in a time where shopping is a pastime to cure things like loneliness and unhappiness. Acquiring things is a status symbol, and yet none of those items can bring the kind of joy Christ freely offers. All you have to do is think of some famous people who seemed to have it all at one time. Greats like writer Oscar Wilde, actor Bela Lugosi, and singer/ actress Judy Garland are reported to have died penniless; however, they'd lived the high life for part of their life. Their temporary wealth was just...well, temporary.

Someone once told me, "This is life and there's just one way out." How true. Every human being on this earth is destined to face his or her mortality one day, although for those who know Christ, it'll be the beginning of a new, wonderful, and perfect eternal existence with Him.

So put away the dollar bills and credit cards. The real treasure that Jesus Christ offers is totally free! ✳ *AKB*

Today's Prayer

Lord Jesus, help us to realize that You are everything,
the beginning and the end, the first and the last,
and the Author and Finisher of our faith.
We praise You for Your incredible gifts,
and we accept them in all humility.
In Your name we pray, amen.

Loving the Unlovable

A new commandment I give to you,
that you love one another;
as I have loved you, that you also love one another.

JOHN 13:34 NKJV

I'd been looking forward to this particular Saturday afternoon for weeks: my two favorite girlfriends and me, three bottomless cappuccinos, a bistro table by the window, and a whole afternoon to catch up. But we'd no sooner exchanged greetings and stirred our coffee when...

"Sandie! How are you, darlin'?"

The hair on the back of my neck stood up and saluted, the way it always did when this particular woman called me "darlin'." We'd worked together for three years, sat in cubicles only a few feet apart, and had the same lunch break schedule. Five days a week, fifty weeks per year, this woman was right in my face! When we were told that our office was being closed down for fiscal reasons and everyone else was crying and worrying about their futures, I was basking in an odd sense of relief. It wasn't that I never wanted to see her again; I just didn't want to see her every single day.

Or on this one.

"Can I join you guys?"

What was I going to say? I could tell from my girlfriends' expressions what they wanted me to say, but I just couldn't do it. And so I uttered the two most unexpected, unfortunate words in the English language: "Of course."

It was admittedly not the most pleasant hour of my life, sitting at that table with my two friends and my former coworker. I wanted to be talking about Jenny's adoption experience and Diana's recent trip to Ecuador. I wanted to hear about all the things I'd missed in the weeks when we'd been too busy to get together. But the truth is...it really wasn't so horrible, either.

This woman contributed to our conversation; she even cracked us up a time or two. A few weeks later, Diana suggested including her on a night out for dinner and a movie. It was only then that I fully realized how much I might have missed by excluding her from our group on that Saturday afternoon, how much my friends might have missed by not having the opportunity to get to know her. And what about how she would have felt if I'd turned her away?

Love one another. It's such a simple command that our Lord left us with, asking us to just love others the way we've been loved. But how many times a day do we miss the opportunity to do just that? How many times do we deprive someone else of the love we have to give?

What's even more important, though, is this: How many times do we deprive ourselves of the opportunity to love someone else for no other reason than to follow the command we were given, the Great Commission, to spread the love around? ✳ *SDB*

Today's Prayer

Father, forgive me for the many times I forget that You have created each and every one of us in this world. Your hand has formed the lovable and the unlovable alike, and Your heart has a place for every person on every corner of this earth. Help me today to share Your love with every life that crosses my path. In the holy name of Jesus I pray, amen.

The Hands (and Feet) of Time

*To every thing there is a season,
and a time to every purpose under the heaven.*

ECCLESIASTES 3:1 KJV

I'm a bit of a history buff, so whenever it seems I'm letting the clocks in my house rule me, I try to dwell on the words of Winston Churchill. Uttered during a World War II meeting with Franklin D. Roosevelt and Joseph Stalin, he said, "What are we? Just specks of dust that have settled in the night on the map of the world."

I'm a neatnik by nature, so the idea that every human being inhabiting the earth can be viewed as a speck of dust instantly transports my mind from a fixation on time to wondering how many cans of Pledge it'll take to clean up *that* mess!

Good old Plautus understood, as early as 200 BC, what a serious conundrum it is—this importance we humans put on the passage of time. "When I was a boy," he wrote, "my belly was my sundial—one more sure, truer, and more exact than any of them. This dial told me when 'twas proper time to go to dinner, when I had ought to eat. But nowadays, why even when I have, I can't fall to unless the sun gives me leave. The town's so full of these confounded dials, the greatest part of its inhabitants shrunk up with hunger, creep along the streets."

Imagine how flustered the poor fella would be if he lived in *our* time, with clocks in every room and on TV channel selectors, caller IDs, and cell phones! What amazing prose might he pen if he heard what we so often say to one another: "If only I had more time..." "Oh, please just give me a minute!" "Goodness but the time flies!" "I haven't a moment to spare." "Um, do you have a second?" Father Time, it seems, rules the world along with everything and every*one* in it!

I often joke about what I consider a serious lack of time by saying, "If only there were forty-eight hours in every day!" But that implies our God has erred, by doling out too few hours. And really, who can know the mind of God?

We're reminded over and over in scripture that God knew *precisely* what He was doing, meting out the days, weeks, and years of His creation. Psalm 90:1–2 tells us He embraces eternity and that He's the Master and Creator of time. Science backs this up in the first and second laws of thermodynamics: Energy and matter cannot be created or destroyed by man, and whatever decays can never all be replaced.

We're stuck, it seems, between the proverbial rock and hard place... the meat in a "deal with it" sandwich. Since only God knows the number of days He intends for us to spend on planet Earth, the best we can do is pray we'll make the best use of our time here. ✳ *LL*

Today's Prayer

Teach me, Father, to recognize every morning as a heavenly gift.
Help me rejoice in the day's precious moments, and give me a grateful heart
that recognizes the power bestowed with each tick of the clock.
Bless me with the wisdom to know the difference between "not wasting time"
and "spending time glorifying Your name." Amen.

What If?

To me, who am less than the least of all the saints, this grace was given,
that I should preach among the Gentiles the unsearchable riches of Christ....
EPHESIANS 3:8 NKJV

I hate to admit this, but I sometimes lie awake at night and wonder "what if."

What if I'd been more obedient to my parents? What if I'd apologized to that friend in high school—the one I turned my back on when she needed someone to talk to? What if I'd actually majored in something more substantial in college? What if I'd been nicer in the grocery store and let the exhausted mother of tots go ahead of me at the deli? What if I'd stopped to pick up that scared, lost puppy on the side of the road? What if I'd turned off my favorite TV show to listen to my daughter tell about her day?

Yeah, I have regrets. I have the desire to do what God calls me to do, but I slip up every single day. I need to do better, but no matter how much nicer and more compassionate I become, it's still not good enough. Does this mean I should hang my head and worry some more? Should I run through my laundry list of what-ifs and wring my hands?

No.

Regrets are burdensome. They weigh on our minds and hearts and give us plenty of reasons to stay in bed all day.

Fortunately, God gave us Christ to wipe away any sins that we might regret. Knowing that the Lord has forgiven us should bring us a peace that's impossible without Him. We're rich with God's grace and mercy.

Knowing that I'm a sinner from birth can be frustrating. However, I have no doubt that I'll be with the Lord for eternity, without an ounce of help from me. He did it all.

The only thing I can do is use my agonizing memories to remind me of how lost I'd be without Him. I don't deserve this wonderful blessing, but because I'm a child of God, I have His love and the promise of eternal life with Him. What a beautiful gift!

I think I'll resolve to focus more on God's grace than all the what-ifs that bog me down. ✳ DM

Today's Prayer

Forgive me for the times I allowed my regrets to place such a heavy burden
on my life that I lost sight of You. I pray that I can cheerfully accept
Your grace with a humble spirit and constant thankful attitude.
Continue to show Your love so I won't lose sight of Your holiness. Amen.

*A*ndrea Boeshaar has been married for more than thirty years. She and her husband, Daniel, have three adult sons, three daughters-in-law, and two precious grandchildren.

Andrea has been writing stories and poems since she was a little girl; however, it wasn't until 1984 that she started submitting her work for publication. In 1991, she became a Christian and realized her calling to write exclusively for the Christian market. Since then Andrea has published articles and devotionals as well as novels and novellas. She recently wrote *Love Finds You in Miracle, Kentucky* for Summerside Press.

In addition to her writing, Andrea speaks at writers' conferences and various women's groups. She is also a cofounder of the American Christian Fiction Writers (ACFW) organization. For many years she served on both its advisory board and as its CEO.

For more about Andrea, visit her Web site at www.andreaboeshaar.com.

*F*or more than a decade, Sandra D. Bricker lived in Los Angeles and, while writing during every spare moment, worked as a personal assistant and publicist to some of daytime television's hottest stars.

She published books and articles for years before entering the inspirational market in 2008. "I'm a Christian woman, first and foremost," she says. "So when Summerside Press chose me as one of two authors to launch their new Love Finds You line, it was a dream come true."

Love Finds You in Snowball, Arkansas was a romantic comedy recognized by three readers' choice awards and countless great reviews. Upcoming laugh-out-loud titles include *Love Finds You in Holiday, Florida; The Big Five-OH!;* and *Always the Baker, Never the Bride*.

Readers can contact her at www.SandraDBricker.com.

*J*esus found **Loree Lough** when, at 26, she attended a friend's church. The sermon that day inspired Loree to accept the Lord as her Savior.

At last count, Loree had 75 award-winning books, with 6 more slated for 2009–2012 release. Her work has also appeared multiple times on CBA best-seller lists and in short stories and articles.

For Summerside Press, she's penned *Love Finds You in Paradise, Pennsylvania* and *Love Finds You in North Pole, Alaska*, with *Love Finds You in Folly Beach, South Carolina* yet to come.

Loree splits her time between an Allegheny mountain cabin and a home in the Baltimore suburbs with her real-life hero-husband and a big clumsy rescue dog named Cash.

To learn more about Loree, visit www.loreelough.com, where you can register to win free copies of her books or kick back with a cup of tea and her latest newsletter.

*A*uthor and speaker **Debby Mayne** grew up in a military family, which meant moving often throughout her childhood. Debby was born in Alaska and has lived in Mississippi, Tennessee, Oregon, Florida, Hawaii, and Japan. She and her husband Wally have two grown daughters, Lauren and Alison, a son-in-law, Jason, and a granddaughter named Emma Grace.

Debby has published more than 25 books and novellas, including *Love Finds You in Treasure Island, Florida* for Summerside Press. She was the managing editor of a national health magazine, a product information writer for a TV retailer, and a copy editor and proofreader for several book publishers.

Today, Debby enjoys writing Christian fiction, which allows her the freedom to tell stories without restraining her convictions. She lives on Florida's west coast with her husband and two cats. To learn more about Debby, visit her Web site at http://debbymayne.com.